YOUR PURPOSE JOURNEY

EMBRACE THE PROCESS

IRENE MUREITHI
AND
JOHN STANKO

UrbanPress
INTERNACIONAL

Your Purpose Journey
by Irene Mureithi and John Stanko
Copyright ©2023 Irene Mureithi and John Stanko
ISBN 978-1-63360-252-6

All rights reserved. This book is protected under the copyright laws of the United States of America. This book may not be copied or reprinted for commercial gain or profit.

For Irene Mureithi's entries, unless otherwise noted, Scripture quotations are taken from the Amplified Bible Copyright © 2015 by The Lockman Foundation, La Habra, CA 90631. All rights reserved.

For John Stanko's entries, unless otherwise noted, Scripture quotations are taken from THE HOLY BIBLE: New International Version ©1978 by the New York International Bible Society, used by permission of Zondervan Bible Publishers. All rights reserved.

Scripture quotations marked NKJV are taken from the New King James Version®. Copyright© 1982 by Thomas Nelson, Inc. Used by permission. All rights reserved.

Scripture quotations marked KJV are taken from the King James Version and rest in the public domain.

Scripture quotations marked NASB are taken from the New American Standard Bible®, Copyright © 1960, 1971, 1977, 1995, 2020 by The Lockman Foundation. All rights reserved.

Scripture quotations marked NLT are taken from the Holy Bible, New Living Translation, copyright © 1996, 2004, 2015 by Tyndale House Foundation. Used by permission of Tyndale House Publishers, Inc., Carol Stream, Illinois 60188. All rights reserved.

For Worldwide Distribution
Printed in the USA

Urban Press
P.O. Box 8881
Pittsburgh, PA 15221-0881
412.646.2780
urbanpress.us

TABLE OF CONTENTS

IRENE MUREITHI

DEDICATION	**V**
ACKNOWLEDGMENTS	**IX**
INTRODUCTION	**XV**
Chapter Two **THE HILTON HOTEL**	**10**
Chapter Three **GROWING UP IN KENYA**	**18**
Chapter Four **TRANSITION AND LIFE AFTER THE BANK**	**28**
Chapter Six **THE LEAN YEARS**	**50**
Chapter Seven **PURPOSE INSIGHTS**	**56**
Chapter Nine **THE PROCESS OF CHANGE FOR PDI**	**77**

JOHN STANKO

INTRODUCTION	**XXIV**
Chapter One **MY PURPOSE JOURNEY**	**1**
Chapter Five **MY PURPOSE STORY**	**43**
Chapter Eight **PERSONALITY**	**69**
Chapter Ten **CREATIVITY**	**89**
Chapter Eleven **THE MONDAY MEMO**	**97**
Chapter Twelve **THE FUNNEL PROCESS**	**111**
Chapter Thirteen **THE FEAR FACTOR**	**118**
CONCLUSION	**127**

DEDICATION

Irene Mureithi

I dedicate this book to every person who desires to live a purpose-driven life.

You may be where I was in March 2007, a season when I desperately needed clarity to the question "Why am I here?" My prayer is that you will find this much-needed clarity once and for all. I found peace and joy that are indescribable when I could say with certainty, "I was born to unlock human capital based on Kingdom principles," which is my purpose statement. May yours be that clear and I dedicate the material in this book to help make that happen.

Maybe your purpose is clear and what you need is boldness to move from an environment that hinders the fulfillment of your purpose. Allow me to share this with you written on Wednesday, 31st October 2007, 5:09p.m. EAT.

Something must die before we can live.

I hugged a few of my colleagues, said the last silent prayer, felt the fear, and did it anyway – walking away from the comfort zone of the banking industry where I had been employed for ten years.

YOUR PURPOSE JOURNEY

Today as I write this, I observed a moment of silence. I have "died many times" in the last 16 years in pursuit of my divine assignment (purpose).

Let no one fool you, for when Apostle Paul wrote "I die daily," he knew something about plugging into his divine assignment.

I am certain that there is a reason why the Master Himself gave us the instructions (not suggestion), "If anyone would come after me let him deny himself, take up his cross daily and follow me" (Matthew 16:24).

You cannot think about the cross without thinking about death. This is not to scare you who wish to embrace a purpose-driven life, but let no one kid you that it's all rosy. There are moments of great joy and deep satisfaction, but there are moments of "death to self" too. I have found both great joy and pain in the purpose journey – and many seasoned purpose seekers will bear witness to what I say. We have all enjoyed days of beautiful sunshine, but that doesn't cancel out the realities of clouds and harsh storms.

On 1st November 2023, I begin my seventeenth year in my PurposeQuest as my purpose coach Dr. John Stanko would call it. There are things I have learned the *hard* way, mainly for lack of knowledge. My desire is that you won't have to learn the hard way like I did. This is why we have written this book. Your journey is unique. However, may you glean from my failures, mistakes, and success stories – authentically shared – as you turn every page.

For those who are experienced in their

purpose journey, more grace as you continue to handhold others. They need your support. Do not hesitate to give it. I am a product of God's amazing grace and all the mentorship, coaching, and training that has graciously been extended to me. It's always a joy to pay it forward.

It is with much love that I dedicate this book to you. I pray that you will fulfill your God-given purpose on this side of eternity. May God's grace abound to you in season and out of season. May you one day hear the Master say to you, "Well done, good and faithful servant! You have been faithful with a few things, I will put you in charge of many things. Come and share your master's happiness!"

ACKNOWLEDGMENTS

To the Father of my spirit, the Shepherd and Overseer of my soul, the Purpose Giver: There are no words to describe my eternal gratitude for the miracle of my birth. Before You formed me in my mother's womb, You knew me. Before I was born, You set me apart. You appointed me as a prophet to the nations. You are my Creator and Maker. You have called me by name. You have ransomed me. You have loved me with an everlasting love. I am all Yours – be it unto me according to Your word – each day as I seek to obey you and fulfill the divine assignment that you have graciously entrusted to me. God the Father, God the Son, and God the Holy Spirit, it's a great honor and privilege to serve Your purposes in my generation. I surrender all.

I am a people person. I love to acknowledge and honor people while they are still alive. I am an advocate of "give people their flowers" while they can still enjoy the scent. For this reason, kindly indulge me. There are so many wonderful people I would like to thank – and this could turn into another book. I will try and keep it short and hopefully in the next book, I can include more names. Feel loved, honored, and appreciated, even if your name is not featured below. You matter to Him and have a divine assignment from God Himself. I acknowledge you. I am rooting for you too!

To my precious Grandmother Milcah Wanjiru Mwarari, who as I write is 93 years young. Thank you so much Cucu (Grandma) for being my prayer partner and a source of daily encouragement. I am convinced the faith that dwells in your heart dwells in mine too. You are a great symbol of patient perseverance. Your love for the Lord throughout my life has been a beautiful thing to behold. Thank you for your joyful spirit. Your laughter makes me laugh even in the hard times. I love you dearly.

My beloved Mother Frashia Wanja – the most loving and selfless soul that I know. Thank you Mommy for your love. I feel it. I know it. I have never doubted it even for a second. I see it in your eyes and I hear it in your words when you say "My daughter" or "Baby Irene." We both know that it has taken the grace of God for you to still be here with us. When the doctors declared "only four months to go" in 2016, we trusted Jesus – and by the stripes that wounded Him you were healed. May you continue to enjoy many more years – and may you continue to age gracefully. You have become more beautiful with each passing day. Much love, Mum!

To my sister, Judy Bradley, what a perfect gift of a sister I have in you. Thank you for your amazing financial support over the years, not only to me but to our entire family. You have literally laid down your life for us. Thank you, Sis, for the love and care. We are so different in our personality styles and that has its fair share of joy and "fight" on the bad days. It is said that "nobody fights you like your own sister, nobody else knows the most vulnerable parts of you and will aim for them without mercy." I can hear you laughing and arguing about this quote despite the many miles that separate us. I love you so very much, Sis! Your sense of fashion is classic! May all your dreams come true. In my love always.

To the most handsome and intelligent young man in my world, Dennis Williams – I love you. I am proud of you. I believe in you. What an adventure it's been the last twenty-four years of God's amazing grace! My heart is filled with many precious memories – and as I write this, I can vividly recall us driving together, just the two of us on Uhuru Highway in your second year of your secondary school, when you told me "my purpose is to give hope." May you continue to fulfill your purpose through all the creative ways in which you are gifted: music, photography, content management, and all the other exciting things that you will continue to discover about yourself as you grow. I also remember how accurately you would share the Word of God with me just when I needed it the most. May you continue to find favor with God and man. I love you forever.

My purpose coach, Dr. John Stanko – I am eternally indebted. "Thank you for giving to the Lord, I am a life that was changed. Thank you for giving to the Lord. I am so glad you gave." These lyrics flood my heart every time I think about you and your support in the last 16 years and counting. God bless you, Sir.

My mentor, Coach Sally Mahihu – what a bond of divine destiny love and support since 2005 when you launched my book titled *Celebrate The Hard Times*. I don't know anyone who is not family who loves me the way Coach Sally does! Many people who admire me in my assignment don't know that if there was a poster child of rejection, I am the perfect candidate, save for the love of God, family and the love, affirmation, support and being "spoiled" by a God-given mentor.

Thank you for allowing God to open doors for me through you. Thank you for inviting me to your high end circles, and always saying to me, "When you get to the venue, tell them you are seated at the table with me." Thank you for inviting me to your book club when I was 31 years young, which was a game changer! I am so thankful to have such a seasoned mentor in you – 18 years and counting by the grace of God.

To my spiritual authority, Rev Teresia Wairimu Kinyanjui of Faith Evangelistic Ministry (FEM). It's an incredible honor to be under your spiritual leadership and effective spiritual oversight since I joined FEM Family Church in 2005. Actually, even joining FEM was a prayer answered since the days I would listen to your teachings through cassette tapes at the age of 14 years in the village. At that tender age, God used you to set my young heart on fire for the Kingdom of God.

I loved and admired the way you taught God's word – with authority and conviction. Even as a teen, I started to sense the difference between religious teachings and faith-filled teachings as I listened to the cassette tapes. Later on in my college days, joining the multitude of believers at Uhuru Park for the crusades was absolutely amazing. I saw the demonstration of the power of God, signs, and miracles, and I became totally sold out to the power of His resurrection!

Thank you so very much for your love, prayers, prophetic words, and for being an example to emulate. Your spirit of excellence has shaped me in many ways. I am a beneficiary of the grace of God that's upon your life and ministry – and for this I am eternally grateful to God and to you too. Thank you very much.

To Bishop Kennedy Kimiywe, thank you, Sir, for your mentorship over the last 18 years. I am indebted for the support that you accorded me. When I launched my first book in 2005, I sent complimentary copies to many servants of God seeking an opportunity to introduce the book to their congregations. You were the only one who responded and invited me to one of the CITAM assemblies that you were pastoring then. I shared my testimonial in the main service briefly and sold books after the service. I kept seeking counsel on how to transition from the bank job into my purpose and all you would say is "Irene, it shall be well" and then pray for me. I became frequent to the point of many people thinking I was a CITAM member.

When I was about to start the Personal Development Institute, one day after driving to more than six venues looking for a place to hold the PDI classes, I parked somewhere, exhausted and gave you a phone call. To cut a long story short, you asked me to drive to CITAM Valley Road – and through your leadership, the church was gracious enough to sublet us a small room near the basketball pitch. That is where PDI classes were launched on 7th April 2010. We conducted the classes from there for a number of years. Thank you so much for all your wise counsel over the years.

To the PDI and TKC community: Thank you very much for allowing me to serve you over the years. I love and appreciate you all. Thank you too for plugging into the divine vision that God has given us.

Special gratitude to my co-founder, Dr. Emma Karari, along with the board of directors and all the TKC leaders. May God bless you in ways that only He can.

And to all my online and offline friends who have cheered me on over the years – thank you. You kept me going in the tough times.

INTRODUCTION

Irene Mureithi

This book is a dream come true. In fact, my entire journey where purpose is concerned has been a dream, a good one for the most part. I have heard Dr. Stanko say that purpose is the only thing that's too good to be true but it's true. When you are in your purpose, you get to do what you love to do as often as possible. In this book, Dr. Stanko and I want to tell you about *Your Purpose Journey: Embrace the Process*. The fact that I get to work on this with my beloved purpose coach is just another wonderful byproduct of my pursuit-of-purpose story.

I want to share my story so people can understand the process and not have unrealistic expectations or abandon the search when the going gets difficult – and it will get difficult. That doesn't mean your journey will be exactly like mine, but you can glean from my journey, and Dr. Stanko's journey, as we co-author this book.

In terms of my professional career, I am a certified life, growth and leadership coach who also heads the Personal Development Institute (PDI) and The Kingdom Connect (TKC) in Kenya.

YOUR PURPOSE JOURNEY

At PDI, we conduct corporate training on emotional intelligence, communication and conflict resolution, change management, among others. We also offer various group and individual coaching sessions, training and mentorship programs on purpose discovery, and personality assessments (DISC).

DISC represents the acronym denoting the four primary personality profiles:

- Individuals displaying *D-type* traits often exude self-assuredness and prioritize achieving tangible outcomes.

- Those with an *I-type* disposition are known for their openness and prioritize fostering connections and the art of convincing and inspiring others.

- *S-type* personalities are renowned for their reliability and prioritize cooperative efforts and genuine sincerity.

- *C-type* individuals prioritize excellence, precision, mastery, and skill in their approach.

We briefly describe them below and hope that you can already tell where your personality lies: I am passionate about helping people to discover their purpose, just like Dr. Stanko helped me to discover mine.

In terms of faith, I'm Kingdom-minded. The Kingdom is an important concept for me because I see it as the opposite of being religious. I accepted Jesus Christ at the age of 14 and received the baptism of the Holy Spirit at that age too. Even though I lived in the village, and without a lot of teachings on the Kingdom, there was something in me that said there had to be a difference between how I saw church being done (like women sitting on one side and men sitting on the other side even while they were married) and how God intended marriage to be.

When I came to the Lord, something in me started questioning what I can now label religious practices. Now that I am more mature and have a better biblical understanding, I'm passionate to see the Kingdom of God being established in the lives of believers. After all, Jesus came preaching the Kingdom and not religion, as it written in Matthew 4:17:

> "From that time Jesus began to preach and say, "Repent [change your inner self—your old way of thinking, regret past sins, live your life in a way that proves repentance; seek God's purpose for your life], for the kingdom of heaven is at hand."

In 2021, PDI launched The Kingdom Connect (TKC) program to share in detail the good news of the Kingdom in the marketplace. This movement has since grown and has close to 1,000 members across 26 counties in Kenya and in the diaspora.

Purpose is really a Kingdom matter for the King is the one who assigns your purpose, and He needs no one's permission to do so—only your cooperation. Dr. Stanko and I have found that the Church is still growing in its receptivity to the purpose message. Most people have heard that they have a purpose, but how to clarify that purpose has remained a mystery, causing frustration in the marketplace and in some churches.

People need to know what the Kingdom of God is and what it is not. Looking back, when I was a new believer, I didn't even know that I was in God's Kingdom until I read Dr. Myles Munroe's book in 2005, *Rediscovering the Kingdom of God*. I feel like without discovering that we are in the Kingdom, we vastly limit God and our purpose. Dr. Stanko has posted on Facebook that the Kingdom is bigger than the Church. The church is part of the Kingdom, but the church is not the Kingdom in its entirety.

Believers who serve God in the marketplace are part of the Kingdom. In fact, Jesus spent more time in the marketplace than He did in the synagogue during His earthly ministry. He recruited marketplace leaders such as fishermen (among them, Peter, James, Andrew and John), a tax collector (Matthew), a doctor (Luke), an activist (Simon the Zealot), and even a thief (Judas)!

People in the marketplace do not just make money. They are on a mission and a divine assignment to spread the gospel in their places of work. They also give their resources to the church to advance the mandate of the Great Commission. Business is where everyday ministry is required and truly happens. We get to reach more people there who don't know the Lord than in the gathered church. We get to interface with people in more real-life situations than those happening in a gathered church a few hours a week. "Occupy until I come" is a greater reality in the scattered church in the marketplace.

We need a better understanding of the fact that the gathered church and the scattered church in the marketplace are one and the same thing. Has the church empowered the marketplace minister to look at business and career from the point of view that they are anointed to be in the marketplace, the same way a minister is anointed to be at the pulpit? The dichotomy between Sunday and Monday has been a flawed understanding from where I sit and work.

Socially, I am single and in my late forties, and trusting God for a Kingdom-minded spouse. In terms of parenting, I've had the joy of bringing up Dennis, a handsome and intelligent young man, for the last 24 years. I'm also honored to care for my mom and my 93-year-old grandmother as they enjoy their glorious sunset years.

This book is my desire to share my life journey, and especially the part where I found and am fulfilling my purpose, so I can encourage and equip others to find their purpose, and live happy and fulfilled lives. By that I mean they can derive the joy that comes from living out their life's purpose. As Dr. Stanko has taught us, one of the greatest byproducts or characteristics of purpose is the joy it brings. It's not about money, prestige, or promotions, although these things often follow and flow from an understanding of our purpose.

Purpose is what helps us to navigate the frustrations that we face in the marketplace. There are people who are doing well financially, yet feel a deep sense of discontent because they lack clarity of their purpose. I've also come across people who are doing very well in their careers, but are unhappy because the roles they play are not aligned to their purpose. The businesses or careers provide the money they need to feed their families, but little in the way of fulfillment.

One of the main reasons for writing this book is to assure people that they can indeed find and live out their purpose. This book will help people understand that purpose is a journey leading to a place that's too good to be true, but it is. That said, the purpose quest comes with its fair share of trials. Sit back and glean from Dr. Stanko's and my journey.

This book is also what I am calling a legacy goal. Writing this book together is like sharing the stage with Dr. Stanko, which I have done many times in person and through the media. I know the two of us will bring a balanced view and approach to the topic of purpose. Our age and gender difference, along with our purpose work in two different cultures, can only enhance our ability to communicate and share.

It's normal in an Introduction to share what the reader can expect in the pages that follow and I want you to know that you can anticipate what I would refer to as transparent authenticity. Both Dr. Stanko and I are authentic. We will share our real-life stories and you can expect that we are not sharing five points to find purpose. Instead, we will be sharing out of our life's journey – the good, the bad, and the ugly, so to speak. And we will share with a view toward equipping you to be a person of purpose like we are.

You may already be familiar with how Dr. Stanko and I came together and I will share more of the story in greater detail later in this book. It was in March of 2007 when we did my DISC assessment at the now-closed Hilton Hotel in Nairobi. I cannot compare what I paid for this session in 2007 to what I have made over the years, and also the joy that this has given me despite the challenges that have been there. My story makes an excellent case study for why coaching is a sound investment with tangible returns. These returns include personal fulfilment, building capacity, increased impact, influence, and income.

Part of my purpose finds its expression in the business of coaching and training. There have been challenges and I must share them with you or else I forfeit the right to call this book and our presentation authentic and transparent. Some were genuine mistakes because I was a young entrepreneur. I got myself into a financial crisis because of high recurrent expenditure that is also referred to as overhead.

Someone once said you learn how to make good decisions after making bad ones, and hopefully I have learned and moved on. In fact, my investment coach at Nabo Capital calls my financial mistakes my "learning portfolio." My only regret is that the mistakes were literally in millions of Kenya shillings. I don't want to imagine what the compounded interest would have been had I invested this money instead. Nevertheless, we serve a God of restoration, renewal, and redemption. In the fullness of time, it shall be well.

Part of my learning has included moving from expensive offices to working online. I now have a lean number of staff, even though we are serving more people than before. The pandemic taught – forced me in reality – to work online and that has made a big difference to the bottom line. I think Dr. Stanko will say the same. We currently serve people who reside in 22 different countries through one of our PDI programs – The Kingdom Connect.

Now I can look back and say that I'm happy I failed at times, for I don't think I would have learned any other way. Maybe there was another way, but for me failure has taught me the best lessons. I went from a place of having and making income, to a place of having absolutely nothing. It's been a joy experiencing divine financial provision. God has helped me to slowly but surely become a better steward. My business has turned around and prospered, and I am happy to share these lessons with others.

As I close, there are two things I hope you receive as you read this book.

The first is hope that you can discover (or rediscover) the Kingdom of God and not just feel confused or bound by religion. You were created for a purpose. May this book help you to find and fulfill your purpose in the Kingdom of God. With that, your impact, influence, and hopefully your income will increase.

Then second thing I desire you to take away is an understanding of the importance and value of relationships. I have been working with Dr. Stanko since March 2007. We've never had a major disagreement. We've never even had a minor disagreement. We often look at things differently but that is the strength of our walk and work together. We learn from one another and grow. This is also true for my other coaches and mentors

— relationships that span decades without conflicts. Purpose helps us to rise above petty issues.

We've proven that it's possible to grow and nurture, win-win, purposeful relationships. We have built that relationship with an eye on God's Kingdom, focusing on what God would want. It's not about money or trying to use the other for personal gain. It's about purpose. We serve the message and then the people who are eager to learn from us. That is where there is mutual support and understanding.

>   Irene Mureithi
>   Nairobi, Kenya
>   December 2023

INTRODUCTION

John Stanko

In 2001, I made a significant, and what eventually proved to be a traumatic, life transition. I left a church I had been with for many years and launched out on my own to start what at first was named the Gold Mine Development Corporation (GMDC). No, it was not a mining entity (although I received many emails promoting mining and metallurgy technology). The company was named after my first book, *Life is a Gold Mine: Can You Dig It?* That book focused on what I call the five Gold Mine Principles, which were designed to help people get their resources "out of the ground of their hearts and minds and into their lives."

But my relationship with Kenya began before I made my transition in 2001. In 1998, I came to visit Pastor Don Matheny at Nairobi Lighthouse Church at the recommendation of American pastors who were working in Zimbabwe. I had worked with their leadership teams in Zimbabwe and they felt I could help the church in Nairobi. I made more than a few visits to Nairobi Lighthouse, working with their leadership team, introducing the DISC profile to them, and speaking at their assemblies. Then I got busy and I was needed less at Lighthouse, so I stopped coming to Kenya for a season.

When I made my transition in 2001, the pastor I had been serving before my transition had a lot of ministry opportunities in South Africa, and I was leading teams to visit there. As some church transitions go, mine did not go well. It seems that the leadership felt I had used them to promote my own ministry in southern Africa and the board declared, according to one man who was present, that "John Stanko has used this ministry as his door to Africa and that door is now closed."

That statement struck me as odd because I had always understood that God was the one who opened and closed doors. So even though I lost everything when I left my church and its leader – ministry connections, finances, covering, support, and ministry history – I determined that if God wanted me in Africa, then that is where I would be. Even though I didn't have the money, I financed a trip to come to Africa on my own to visit leaders in Zambia, Zimbabwe, and South Africa.

I remember waking up in my hotel room in Durban on that trip and the Lord's presence was in the room. Of course, I had no idea how I was going to make a living, but I had assumed that if I was going to work in Africa, donors in the United States were going to have to support me. However, on that Durban morning, the Lord spoke to me out of His presence and said, "I will confound your thinking and your critics. You will never leave Africa without dollars or British pounds in your pocket."

And then I made my own declaration, standing on African soil that if God wanted me to be here, and I felt He did, then nothing was going to stop me. I made that bold statement to no one in particular, but I felt I was saying it to principalities and powers, "I can't be intimidated. I did nothing wrong to warrant my transition, but even if I had, God will adjust me and redeem the situation. I'm here to stay." And I must say that God has been true to His word. Rather than people giving to my ministry so I could work in Africa, I have worked in Africa so I could live in the United States!

Right after that I came back to the States and began writing what I titled *The Monday Memo*. When I left my church to start my ministry, I had begun teaching and writing about what I called the Goldmine Principles – purpose, goals, time management, organization, and faith – in 1985. As I became better known for those principles, over the years invitations came to teach them in various church settings, one of which was in Kenya where I had not been for a few years. My good friend, Kentice Tikolo in Kenya, had started receiving *The Monday Memo* based on her cousin's recommendation, and she wrote to see if I was open to coming to Kenya to talk about purpose. She said the country needed to hear it.

I said I would be glad to if I was ever in the region and lo and behold, about a year later I got an invitation to come to Uganda with a team from my hometown. I wrote Kentice and asked her if she thought it would be worthwhile for me to come over to Kenya and she said by all means. So I flew over to Nairobi and Kentice picked me up. That was the first time we met. She took me right to HOPE FM radio where I was interviewed about the purpose message.

Then the next day, I was to be on a show with Tina Nzuki for a few minutes but the interview went so well and the response was so overwhelming that I ended up being on her show all week. From those interviews, I added 1,200 names to my *Monday Memo* mailing list. What's more, Kentice had arranged for me to speak at Nairobi Pentecostal Church on Valley Road for their midweek and Sunday services. I was back in Kenya in a big way.

For the next several years, I would come to Kenya and Kentice would set up seminars, consultations with companies, and one-on-one coaching sessions. It was at one of those seminars where I first met Irene, or I should say she met me. I did not connect with her until our meeting at the Hilton for her personal coaching session, which you will hear all about later in this book. From that time on, Irene became my ardent student, meeting with me regularly, reading and listening to everything I had on the topics of purpose and the DISC profile – another resource you will learn more about later.

I nicknamed Irene "Madame Dynamique" because she was so enthusiastic and dynamic every time I heard her talk, and eventually I gave her the honorary title of "My Best Student in the World." I have had many drink deeply from my purpose material but no one has drawn deeper than Irene. What's more, she has taken the purpose message to new heights, sharing insight from which I and many others have learned. She truly is my best student who is now my peer if not my master.

Irene has been kind enough to include me in many of her business and purpose endeavors. She has honored me in person and in social media as her coach. When I think of Irene, however, I think of the Chinese proverb that says, "When the student is ready, the teacher appears." Irene was ready and I just happened to come along by God's grace to give her what she was looking for – she just didn't know what it was. Now she has her own following and message and I am glad that we are still connected after all these years.

When I first began teaching on purpose in 1991, I knew I was on to something special. My first purpose workshop was at an Integrity Music worship weekend in Pismo Beach, California. I was convinced that no one was going to attend my workshop because, after all, this was a worship conference. Who would want to listen to me talk about "Effectiveness: Finding Your Life Purpose." People did come. During the session, the atmosphere was both sober and electric, if that makes any sense, as people connected with the message.

People actually cried when I spoke about finding purpose (yes, Irene, you were not the only one). I had caused many people to cry in ministry up to that point, but seldom for the right reasons! This, however, was different. They were weeping because the connection with the message touched something deep in their heart. People mobbed me after the session and we decided to offer the workshop two months later in Dallas, Texas. The results were the same, and then we moved on to Cincinnati, Florida, Atlanta, and Memphis. After that, the seminar went international, and I had a chance to test the purpose message with a non-American audience. Was the purpose message an Americanized topic, or would it "translate" into other cultures? Again, I had my doubts, but we found that it did. I delivered the message in Taiwan, Hong Kong, Australia, New Zealand, and Europe. People couldn't get enough of the message, and I was only too happy to oblige.

Yet there was a problem (a fly in the ointment, as an old saying goes), and to me it was a big one. People would cry, laugh, and give me compliments on the message, but when I would ask them, "What do you think your purpose is?", they would often reply, "I have no idea, but the message was so good!" My thought was, *How good can it be if you don't find your purpose?* That caused me to develop probing questions to help people clarify their purpose ("What would you do if you had all the money you needed to live on? What do people give you compliments for that you don't think is very special?"). Then came follow-up articles and essays, additional seminars, and eventually books.

I incorporated the personality profiles into my one-on-one coaching sessions (I found I had to make myself available to schedule those after I taught). That proved to be valuable as a tool to help people, especially Christians, talk about who they are and are not.

When I returned to Kenya in 2004, I had 13 years of experience helping people discover their purpose. I was a "bad purpose dude" (an outdated way to say I was good at what I did) who was getting more confident with each passing year. My connection with Kentice and then Irene was a divine connection and that led us to many exciting experiences and new insights as we worked, talked, counseled, coached, and ministered together. It's been a heavenly connection.

In this book, Irene will share her purpose journey, going back to her childhood. I chose not to go back that far (I am older than Irene, and any recollections would be ancient history). I have decided to start with 1991, touch on 2001, and then bring you into the present. During that time, I changed the name of my business from the Gold Mine Development Company to PurposeQuest Inc., which is the reason I will reference the concept of a purpose quest (sometimes one word) as I go.

Irene will share what she learned about herself through the DISC profile and how the purpose message has set her free – and is still doing so. I am going to share my purpose insights so you understand how and why Irene and I connected so completely around the purpose message. We are convinced that the best of our relationship is yet to come, and that's good news for purpose seekers everywhere.

We hope this book inspires, encourages, enlightens, and informs you. If not, we hope that it at least entertains you, for both of us are known to make people smile – and we love doing that. Along the way, we want to help you connect with us and with the concept we love that changed our

JOHN STANKO

lives. We know as you connect with the purpose message, it will change your life as it did ours.

Dr. John Stanko
Pittsburgh, PA USA
December 2023

Chapter One
MY PURPOSE JOURNEY

John Stanko

Malcolm Gladwell in his book *Outliers* expressed the belief that when someone devotes 10,000 hours of concentrated study or effort in an area or discipline, that person will be an expert or top performer in their field. Author Seth Godin urges his readers to find something they do and perfect it to become one of the best in the world, and then to give their lives to expressing it.

We won't debate whether the premises of these two men are true. I will tell you, however, that I decided to take both men at their word, and I have invested more than 10,000 hours in helping others find purpose because I wanted to be one of the best, and the most skilled and anointed purpose coaches in the world. I will leave the results and the "standings" of where I rank in God's hands, but I have paid the price to be the best I can be.

The years since 1991 have been the most fulfilling of my life as I have traveled to 50 countries to address audiences large and small about purpose. Along the way, I have had one-on-one purpose sessions with thousands of people. I have focused on my own purpose and saw my understanding of it change ever so slightly, but the change released an avalanche of creativity in me that has yet to cease. I've seen many come to a better understanding of who they are and why they're here as I shared my journey and what I've learned about purpose.

We (Irene and I) seldom have anyone challenge us to the validity, worth, or biblical correctness of our purpose presentations. Almost everyone intuitively knows the truth about purpose. Most people familiar with the Bible have at one time or another quoted to someone the words of Romans 8:28: "All things work together for good for those who love God and are called according to His *purpose*" (emphasis added). Perhaps they even know Proverbs 16:4, "The Lord has made everything for its own *purpose*, even the wicked for the day of evil" (NASB, emphasis added).

Many have found that talking about purpose, however, is a lot easier than defining it for themselves in a personal way. Irene and I want to help you get beyond *agreeing* that you have a purpose to the point where you can *clearly state the reason* you were born. We're more convinced than ever before that it's possible for everyone to do that, even you. If Irene and I did it, we came to the conclusion so can you.

In our travels and study, we've met many wonderful people who have the same burden we do: to see people doing not just good things, but the best things they were created for. We've also found that other groups, with differing philosophical perspectives, have pursued this topic and have produced some interesting books and articles, some before we ever started our quest for purpose. For instance, Laurence G. Boldt wrote these words in his book, *How to Find the Work You Love*:

> The quest for the work you love—it all begins with the two simple questions: Who am I? And What in the world am I doing here? While as old as humanity itself, these perennial questions are born anew in every man and woman who is privileged to walk upon this earth. Every sane man and woman, at some point in his or her life, is confronted by these questions—some while but children; more in adolescence and youth; still more at midlife or when facing retirement; and even the toughest customers at the death of a loved one or when they themselves have a brush with death. Yes, somewhere, sometime, we all find ourselves face to face with the questions, Who am I? and What am I here for?
>
> And we do make some attempt to answer them. We ask our parents and teachers, and it seems they do not know. They refer us to political and religious institutions, which often crank out canned answers devoid of personal meaning. Some even tell us that life has no meaning, save for eating and breeding. Most of us are smart

enough to recognize that canned answers or begging the question will not do. We must find real answers for ourselves. But that takes more heart and effort than we are often willing to give.[1]

We agree with much of what Mr. Boldt wrote. We can confirm from our experience that almost everyone faces the issue of purpose at one time or another. You are also, or you wouldn't be reading this book or trying to answer the questions: *Who am I?* and *What am I here for?* People begin their quest for answers at different stages of life, some in childhood and some at retirement. Irene and I want to help you find answers to those questions.

Furthermore, religious institutions (i.e., the Church, of which we are both well acquainted) sometimes offer "canned answers" that leave people with simplistic solutions to their purpose questions: *How can I know God's will for my life? How then can I do it?* Often people tell us they are here "to do the will of God," "to glorify God," "to serve others," or "to worship Him." The problem is that these answers fall short, for you must go further to find the *specific* will of God for your life, *what it is* that will glorify God, *how* you can serve others, and *what it means* to worship God beyond singing a hymn or chorus on Sunday morning.

Since Irene and I became friends and co-workers in the purpose vineyard, we have witnessed the release of the best-selling book in the history of publishing (next to the Bible), Rick Warren's *The Purpose-Driven Life*. Despite Pastor Warren's impact, we still find that people are searching and digging for purpose more

frantically than ever. In a sense, as purpose possibilities have expanded exponentially, it has created another purpose question in people's minds: *With so many options for what I can do, how do I know what I should do?*
The pursuit of answers "takes more heart and effort than we are often willing to give," as Mr. Boldt wrote. It's much easier to settle for pat answers or to have someone else define who we are, but that's like putting a band-aid on a major laceration. It may look good and even cover the wound, but it won't necessarily bring the desired long-term results, clarity, or fulfillment.

It isn't uncommon for those who discuss the topic of purpose to at some point refer to the issue of a life's calling or vocation. The word *vocation* comes from the Latin word *vocare*, which means *to call*. Originally a person could be called or have the vocation of a shoemaker. Eventually a vocation or call became associated with a religious calling to the priesthood or some other form of ministry.

The very concept of a calling means that there is some intelligent force or being doing the calling. We cannot conceive of how an activity can produce a call to a person. A calling presupposes that an intelligent being or force is doing the calling. Our course, from our Christian worldview, we know that a calling comes from someone – God – to someone – His creation.

It's when we seek to serve God and cooperate with His plan that we have found our lives to have meaning and direction. As the psalmist wrote, "My help comes from the Lord, the maker of heaven and earth" (Psalm 121:2). The designer of a thing is the perfect one to define the purpose of the designed, and that is why I look to, even expect, the God of heaven and earth to answer my purpose questions. Mr. Boldt writes,

> Finding the work you love is not a cerebral process. It is not a matter of figuring something out through a process of rational analysis. It is a process of opening yourself and beginning to pay attention to what you respond to with energy and enthusiasm. Pay attention to the people, events, and activities in the outside world that evoke the strongest response from you. Pay attention as well to your inside world, to the inspirations and intuitions that most excite you. From within and without, let yourself be moved. Listen to your own heart and learn to trust what it is saying.[2]

There is a section of the Christian community in Kenya and the world that finds the advice to "listen to your heart" a New Age concept. The argument is based on Jeremiah 17:9, "The heart is deceitful above all things, and desperately sick; who can understand it?"

The problem with this is that we heed the warning in Jeremiah 17:9 without moving on to the next verse, where the Lord answered His own question: "I the Lord search the heart and examine the mind, to reward each person according to their conduct, according to what their deeds deserve" (Jeremiah 17:10). It would seem from the context that God evaluates our heart matters and they can't all be evil, otherwise there would be nothing to reward. God could have said, "I'm going to punish all deeds that emanate from your heart, which is evil and beyond hope." That isn't what He said.

Then we read what David wrote in Psalms 21 and 37. It seems from those verses that there is some remnant of hope for our heart, but how can we know when to trust it? The key is not to stop at what Jeremiah 17:9-10 says, but to read what else the Lord had to say that pertains to the heart. The Lord promised He would do a new thing in our hearts when He introduced a new covenant:

> "The days are coming," declares the Lord, "when I will make a new covenant with the people of Israel and with the people of Judah. It will not be like the covenant I made with their ancestors when I took them by the hand to lead them out of Egypt, because they broke my covenant, though I was a husband to them," declares the Lord. "This is the covenant I will make with the people of Israel after that time," declares the Lord. "I will put my law in their minds and write it on their hearts. I will be their God, and they will be my people" (Jeremiah 31:31-33).

It seems that God promised to override the operating system of our old heart with a new script, new code if you think in computer terminology. Therefore, some things in our hearts may be good, recorded there in God's own handwriting, but that still may mean that we have an old wineskin of a heart and Jesus said new wine can't go into an old wineskin or the skin will burst. God took care of that problem as explained to the prophet Ezekiel:

> "For I will take you out of the nations; I will gather you from all the countries and bring you back into your own land. I will sprinkle clean water on you, and you will be clean; I will cleanse you from all your impurities and from all your idols. I will give you a new heart and put a new spirit in you; I will remove from you your heart of stone and give you a heart of flesh. And I will put my Spirit in you and move you to follow my decrees and be careful to keep my laws" (Ezekiel 36:24-26).

So when David wrote in Psalm 9:1, "I will give thanks to you, Lord, with all my heart," was he offering God a tainted sacrifice of praise because he was doing it with "all my heart"? Of course not. The heart and the head are both important in your search for purpose.

Our desire is to help you listen and be moved to see yourself not as others see you, but as God sees you. We encourage you to record your thoughts or impressions as you read, or jot down cross references that you want to look up later in your journal. As you set your mind and heart to seek your purpose, it's important to pay attention to your thoughts and impressions that are calling out to you. They may not even make sense when you hear them, but it's important that you "honor" them as they come.

Despite the explosion of purpose material, coaches, seminars, books, and movies, people are still asking the questions mentioned earlier. They want to know their purpose. This indicates that much work remains to be done for us to be a purpose-driven people. Irene and I want to share with you what we've learned so you can learn and grow in your own self-awareness. We want to help you as you embark on or continue your purpose quest.

We invite you to connect with us now as we share how our connection with one another and the purpose message has furthered the concept of purpose in the lives of people all over the world. We are confident your connection with the purpose message and with us will give you your own unique stories as well. Let's get started.

Chapter Two
THE HILTON HOTEL

Irene Mureithi

The best way I can describe my life between 2002 and 2007 is Triple B: Bored Beyond Belief. I was working at one of the largest commercial banks in Kenya. I was in operations where I would move from one function to another. I started as a teller, then moved into customer service, and sometimes I would sit in the business development officer's desk. No matter what role I had, all the duties were routine, but the teller job was the most draining.

Before that, I had worked in a foreign exchange bureau at the Jomo Kenyatta International Airport. By 2007, I had nine years of experience between both places. For ordinary Kenyans, these represented good jobs because of the job security. Most bank jobs are pensionable so you could work there until retirement or in a worst-case-scenario, retrenchment.

Today, some of my colleagues who sat in the cubicle next to mine are all bank managers. My family likes to remind me often that I too could have been a bank manager now. The trajectory for me at the bank would have been to grow in the operations and finally into management. Despite the rosy prospects of working a bank job and the accompanying benefits, I was miserable. To some, my discontent bordered on being ungrateful in an environment where many people were jobless. I truly was grateful to God for the job, but my heart was searching for my life's work or purpose.

It was about this time that I heard about a man named John Stanko. I decided to attend a meeting he facilitated at the Nairobi Safari Club. After I heard him teach on purpose, I sought a one-to-one session. I borrowed US$150 for this session from my colleagues. When they asked me what it was for, they laughed hysterically asking me whether I would become the Chief Executive Officer of the bank after the coaching session. They wondered why I was being 'extravagant,' seeking a loan for a session I couldn't afford. To them, this was a light matter. To me, it was a destiny moment. I had a burning desire that the waters of their taunts could not quench!

It was in March 2007 that I went for the one-to-one session with Dr. Stanko. I came to where he was staying at the Hilton Hotel in Nairobi to try and figure out what my purpose in life could possibly be. I was hoping against hope that it wasn't the Triple B!

My time with Dr. Stanko was the first professional coaching session I had ever had. Apart from the insight I was about to receive from my DISC personal assessment, it was refreshing just having someone listen to me without judgment. Any other time when I had tried to tell someone that I didn't like what I was doing, they would always advise me to be thankful to God that I had a job.

It's not that I was not being grateful, I was just confessing that for me the job was very routine. Even when having that conversation with my beloved mother, she always reminded me that I had a mortgage, so there was no way I could even think of leaving that job (just in case my being bored beyond belief was leading me to resign). Over the years, my purpose coach has listened to me without prejudice and it is still very precious to me.

During our session, Dr. Stanko asked the question that changed my life forever. After looking at my DISC profile results, he asked me, "What are you doing in a bank?" He hit the nail on the head. I wanted someone who could tell me to get out! He didn't tell me to do anything like that, but his question was a confirmation of what I had sensed. The bank was not where my calling was. I shouldn't be there.

Dr. Stanko commented that I had a voice for the media. Then we went over the results from my DISC report, and I was able to see that I have an inspiring and influential personality from what the profile refers to as an 'I-D' style. It really spoke accurately to who I am. I felt it was a perfect description of the real me. Over the years, I've heard clients who also attest to the accuracy of their DISC reports. It has helped them to clarify their life purpose just like it did for me.

I had heard Dr. Stanko at the seminar so I expected that he was going to tell me what my purpose was, and I wondered how he would know from just one session. I was eager to see how he was going to help me find my purpose.

I really had not heard of or completed the DISC personality assessment before my session with Dr. Stanko. The results ended up being better than I expected because of the way he used it to guide our discussion of my personality and how it related to what God wanted me to be. He never told me what my purpose was, but I was able to connect the dots by embracing who I was in terms of my personality and through the reflective questions he asked me in the session. His question of what I was doing at the bank could not be answered yes or no. I had to go away from our session and seek the answers. It got me thinking.

My session along with my DISC report helped me see that the bank was not where I was meant to be. And of course, I had the inner witness from the Holy Spirit. However, I had no idea how I was going to get out because I had a mortgage of just over US$30,000 that was still outstanding.

Dr. Stanko informed me he was flying back to the States that evening and promised to send my DISC report. When I left the Hilton, I boarded a *matatu* (public transport) back home with so many thoughts on my mind. I knew I must resign from the bank if I was ever going to fulfil my purpose. However, I remained restless about how I would settle the mortgage. I decided to take a step of faith and wrote a resignation letter that night. I would hand in that letter seven months later in October 2007. Coach Stanko got to the US and emailed me the DISC report as promised. We were not in contact for a number of years after this.

Even though my purpose was not yet crystal clear, there was a sense of freedom in my spirit that I didn't have to stay at the bank forever. I saw the end of the tunnel. Looking back now, I can say that the Hilton session gave me so much hope, even though I couldn't yet connect all the dots. No one can connect them all. As Steve Jobs said, "You can't connect the dots looking forward; you can only connect them looking backwards. So you have to trust that the dots will somehow connect in your future."

In hindsight, when I remember how I cried during the session—and the stares that I got as people wondered what this *mzungu* (Caucasian) had done to cause tears to freely flow down my cheeks. I now understand this is what is called the pain point in coaching. That question, "What are you doing in the bank?", addressed my pain. I learnt something that day and I have Dr. Stanko to thank for the teaching. Purpose and tears are connected.

Whether I teach purpose class online or in person, sometimes people ask for a timeout because the tears just hit them. The purpose conversation has a way of touching the core of any human being. The pain of knowing you were designed for more, yet staying in a constrained environment despite incredible benefits if one were to leave, is a story many professionals and some entrepreneurs can relate to.

The last 13 years as the lead purpose coach at Personal Development Institute have given me the opportunity to have deep conversations with professionals, entrepreneurs, and people working in faith-based organizations who have this cry as well. No amount of money can satisfy the hunger for purpose. As Mark Twain said, "The two most important days in your life are the day you are born, and the day you find out why."

Cam Taylor expounds on Mr. Twain's thoughts by saying that the third most important day is the one when you take action to live out your 'why.' He adds,

> The difference between intention and action is massive. It's not enough to simply spend days, weeks, months, and years contemplating your why. Once you discover it, you must do something to live it out. You may hold back from taking action because of fear, anxiety, past failure, insecurity, or feeling like you're not quite ready. I know the feeling, but to be truly alive and a difference maker, you must stop letting your limiting beliefs and attitudes hold you captive.[3]

Now I understand that when you touch your purpose, you touch the heart of God. He knows your name and has something for you to do that only you can do. It's quite moving when you find out the reason you were born.

While being in the banking industry for the first five years was great, I felt like fish out of water in the other five years. There are days I went to see the doctor only to discover my dis-ease was due to discontentment rather than disease. At some point, I was getting ill when I would approach my workplace because of the stress that I experienced in that building. I would have headaches or just generally feel unwell. This condition is described as a psychosomatic disorder. Many employees go through this disorder silently. The workplace should provide safe spaces where people can talk about these anxieties.

The human resource department should not punish employees who feel this way. They are not disengaged or suffering the usual "Monday Blues." Not everyone needs to resign from their job to find and fulfill their purpose. Some just need upskilling, reskilling, or redeployment within the organization.

For example, had I gotten a chance to work in the learning and development (training) department at the bank, I would have been in my purpose. I actually asked for this opportunity while I was still at the bank, but it was not possible to be redeployed at that point. For organizations that are focused on retaining their best talent, upskilling and reskilling of your workforce is a more cost-effective and mutually beneficial strategy. It creates a happiness culture and makes your company a great place to work.

Today, I get to work with banks and other corporate organizations providing training services. Finally, the dream has come true the long way. I've shared about the meeting that changed my life, but now let me go back and tell you about my life that led to the bank in the first place. You will learn that the seeds of my purpose were present even as a young child, but culture and other expectations didn't allow them to sprout and bear fruit in previous seasons.

Chapter Three
GROWING UP IN KENYA

Irene Mureithi

I was born at the Bondeni Maternity Hospital in Nakuru, which is one of the 47 counties in Kenya. Dr. Stanko and I share many jokes, and one of them is the assumption by some who assume that all Africans are born at home. While it is true that even in modern Kenya there are still home deliveries in some remote areas, the vast majority of Kenyans enjoy decent and affordable maternity services in government health facilities. The middle and upper class have access to world-class services at high-end private hospitals. There is also an emerging trend of people who can afford both government or private services preferring a home birth instead.

I grew up with my mom and grandmother in the village, in an area called Ngecha Farm, Bahati, in Nakuru County. I thank God for my late dad. He was not actively present in my life as I was growing up. As an adult, with the blessing of my Mom, I embarked on a search mission to reconnect with him. I had not seen or heard from him for about 26 years.

In 2005 while still working at the bank I authored my first book titled, *Celebrate the Hard Times*, and I decided to put a copy of the publication in my dad's hands. I felt that some of my hard times were a result of his absence in my life. We reconnected when I was 33 years young and that is also the time I resigned from the bank to pursue my life purpose. I had the privilege of leading my dad to Jesus, and hosting him in Nairobi for a brief stay as he recuperated from a short illness. We remained in touch and I would visit him from time to time. In January 2015, he went home to be with the Lord.

I attended St. John's Primary School from class one through to class eight. I gave my life to Christ at the age of 14, as I had said. I grew up attending two churches. I'd go to the Presbyterian church with Mom, and the Catholic church with my grandmother. Occasionally, I'd go to church with my great grandfather who was an Orthodox Christian.

I observed many differences between the three denominations and several others like the Full Gospel and Anglican Churches, which were all located in the same shopping center. My teenage heart had many questions as to why all these people worshiping the same God had different church 'labels.' My desire to understand the Kingdom of God started here. Thank God that when we rediscover the Kingdom, labels don't apply.

During my Sunday School days, I used to run to the vestry where the elders met before they came into the main sanctuary in the Presbyterian church. I'd always run there and ask permission to recite a Bible verse or a poem in the adult service. When I was denied an opportunity to do so, sometimes I cried and even asked them what was the purpose of coming to church if I couldn't tell God what was in my heart. That is another example of my outgoing, verbal personality playing a role early in my life. As a certified life and growth coach, I now encourage parents to understand their children's personality styles from an early age because these hardly change through the teen and young adult years into adulthood.

Children who are outgoing can be helped to understand this and even harness it towards their careers. Those who are reserved tend to exhibit this style even in adulthood, and it shapes their task-oriented preferences for careers. When we offer the DISC assessment for children from the age of nine, we help parents to understand the career choices of the different children. Some are outgoing and people-oriented, while others are reserved and task-oriented. Why should parents guess and make mistakes when they can have near-accurate reports on their children's personality styles and their possible career paths?

I'm the last born in a family of three girls, so I was pretty much the spoiled one – or so they say. Mom disputes that and doesn't think I was spoiled. She thinks I was very responsible. She says to this day that she never had to chastise me growing up because I was obedient. My sisters would complain about that because they would get disciplined frequently. As adults, we all laugh it off. My sisters say my love for reading kept me out of trouble.

After class eight, I went to Kericho County for my secondary education at Mercy Girls Secondary School, Kipkelion. I was a bright student. Outside of class, I loved the Christian Union and was always a leader in our local chapter, both in primary school, secondary school, and even college.

My pet subjects were English, history, Christian cducation, and home science. I wasn't too much into sports, and just did the basics that every student had to do in terms of physical education. I didn't have a favorite sport or anything like that. I loved debating and won trophies that I've kept to this date. I think the 'I' in me from the DISC profile was affirmed when I debated. I can look back now and understand that my personality and strengths were operating even when I wasn't consciously aware of them.

I was an outgoing child, and when I saw the results of my DISC profile in 2007, I then understood that was, and is, my core personality style. That's why the DISC affirmed me in a very deep place because I was able to look back, even into my childhood, and see then that this is who I have always been. When I completed the DISC profile, I understood, for example, that it's easier for people who have a compliant or C personality, to thrive in a work environment that requires detail orientation and numbers. On the other hand, people who have the 'D' or dominant style find themselves in positions of leadership. Those with the 'S' personality have the steadiness that helps them strike a balance between people and tasks. We recommend that adults invest in their assessment and coaching for in-depth understanding.

Though I attained the B grade required to enroll in either public or private university, my first choice was to St. Paul's United Theological College (now St. Paul's University). I wanted to study theology and become an ordained minister of the gospel. I made an application to the college, but my church elder said I could not become a pastor at that young age. I later ended up at Kenya Utalii College in Nairobi, Africa's leading hospitality and tourism training institute.

I applied for a four-year course in hotel management at the institution and was admitted. Within two months, I changed the course because I felt that was going to be very restrictive and would keep me within the hospitality industry. Again, that now speaks to the 'I' personality even though I didn't have that kind of personal awareness back then. I remember thinking, *With this four-year course, I can only work within the hotel industry. That sounds like I'm going to be in a box. Let me take a two-year front office course which has the potential to expose me to working with hotels, airlines, banks, insurance companies, hospitals, literally anywhere – as long as there's a front desk.*

Parents who have children with an 'I' personality have to be aware that their kids tend to have a big picture mindset from an early age. They also value personal freedom even when their young minds cannot figure out the details of how that plays out in real life. In their world, people come first. Trying to restrict such a child into schedules and the world of detail kills their creativity and morale.

Naturally, the society expects everyone to secure gainful employment in something long-lasting and stable. When I changed my course of studies, the decision did not sit well with my elder sister or Mom because they felt I was letting go of an opportunity for a bigger job. With the four-year program, I could have ended up being a hotel general manager at some point had I pursued that career.

However, that wasn't what I was looking for. I needed something that would be fun and exciting across various industries, instead of being locked into one. Later, I found out through the DISC profiles that a variety of activities helps combat my common frustration – which is boredom with the ordinary. Again, I was thinking, *Why not work for five years, maybe in a bank, and then another five years at the airlines?* At one point, I applied for a cabin crew role with our national carrier, Kenya Airways, but my height kept my dreams on the ground. Luckily, I have taken to the skies with different airlines as I fulfil my purpose across the nations.

I hope my stories will encourage someone not to give up on their dreams. God has a way of giving us the desires of our hearts in a version that may vary from our original ideas, but it ends being the same thing – the dream of flying to the nations has been fulfilled, but not as cabin crew!

Mathematics was not one of my pet subjects. While I scored an overall B-minus in my high school exit examination, I got a 'D' in Math. In an interesting twist, I ended up working in the bank handling billions in all the major global currencies. I encourage children to work hard and score the best possible grade in all subjects. However, parents should not diminish their children's worth and potential based on grades. As we all find out later as adults, there's more to life than grades. Values, character, purpose, and passion help you to stay grounded and attain sustainable success long after the national exams.

It's sad to see young people in Kenya commit suicide because of getting what the society perceives to be poor grades. I believe there is goodwill in Kenya government's introduction of the Competency Based Curriculum (CBC) despite its implementation challenges.

People need help to understand who they are and who they're not, and that's the reason that much of my business focus right now is to help children, teenagers, and young adults to understand how they are wired, because most of the time people don't change. This also involves educating their parents to this reality. As a matter of fact, when we conduct the children's DISC assessment, many of them ask us whether their parents can also take the personality profile.

Upon completion of my two-year front office studies, I graduated and immediately got a job at the Jomo Kenyatta International Airport working for a foreign exchange bureau. I was a forex teller, so I was handling a lot of global currencies. It was a good experience since I grew up in the village, but there I was at an international airport interacting with people from all over the world.

A lot of my dreams about traveling were birthed in that season – though I could not see where I would be traveling to.

Every time I travel to spread the purpose message, I'm always grateful. Purpose is that thing that opens doors for people and it certainly did for me. Basically, I was just handling cashier duties at my first job. Planes full of people were landing and everyone was looking to exchange their currency for the Kenya shilling, and then doing the same when they left to change shillings back into their home currency. There wasn't much to do apart from that.

You may wonder how my travel dreams were developed there when I sat in a cubicle all day and changed money. I would sit and listen to all the flight announcements every day and wonder why someone was going to Dubai. Why were they going to Uganda? What are they going to do there? Who are they? My global perspective was formed there listening to the airport intercom directing passengers to different boarding gates. God never wastes our experiences.

This may sound unusual, but God also used that job to help shape my abundance mentality. I handled so much money from many countries, and it convinced me that there was money in circulation. I learned there was a lot of money in the world and that made me wonder why my boss was giving me so little as a salary.

Let me go back and tell you how the Christian part of my life came to be. There were actually two instances when I gave my life to Christ at the age of 14. One was an altar call in church in the village when I gave my life to Christ. Then the same year when I was 14, I came to Nairobi to visit my auntie. I thought because I had told a lie here and there that maybe I was no longer born again. So I asked my auntie to lead me to the Lord again, which she did. So those are the two instances that I give my life to Christ, both at the age of 14.

In the village when I was first born again, I also experienced the baptism of the Holy Spirit, which was very strange because the Presbyterian Church at that time did not emphasize the gift of speaking in tongues. However, I had read a lot about it in the book of Acts, so when it happened to me, I didn't think it was strange. Some church leaders questioned the infilling of the Holy Spirit. At that that point they began telling Mom that I needed to leave the church. It didn't make sense to me because I saw it in the Bible, wanted it, asked God for it and received it, only to find out the church didn't agree with me – or the Bible!

Before I was born again, I would often read the Word. That's part of the reason I desired to be born again. It must have been the Holy Spirit at work. I didn't know why, but I had often read the book of Acts. Now I know that the Holy Spirit was preparing me for His baptism. I was involved in youth leadership in my church even before the age of 14, so I just continued to serve. Maybe the only noticeable change after my surrender to Christ was my keen awareness of what I would increasingly identify as the differences between the Kingdom of God as opposed to religion. I noticed things in religion, and they would bother me. The written word of God is the final authority in a believer's life, and this should be taught in all churches so that the saints are aligned to the Kingdom of God instead of religious dogma.

For the two years I was in college, I was part of an in-house college church, the Christian Union (CU), in which I was a leader. Occasionally I would go to other churches to which I was invited. Then I started attending monthly crusades by Evangelist Teresia Wairimu of Faith Evangelistic Ministry (FEM) at Nairobi's Uhuru Park in 1994. I first heard of her teachings through cassette tapes in the village when I was 14, and desired to connect in person though I didn't know how it would ever happen.

It was at Uhuru Park that I first saw the demonstration of the power of God. Evangelist Wairimu was mentored by the late Evangelist Reinhard Bonnke, whose legendary miracle crusades would attract millions of people in Africa. The life, work, and ministry of Evangelist Bonnke are known worldwide.

As Evangelist Wairimu preached at Uhuru Park, I finally saw somebody who believed what the Bible said was still possible today. I witnessed the sick being healed among many other miracles. In 2005 I started attending the weekly Sunday services at FEM Family Church in Karen, Nairobi. That is where I go to church up to this day. I am greatly honored to sit and learn under one of the most seasoned and accurate prophets in our generation. I thank God for her spiritual leadership. I have enjoyed support from the woman of God, our pastors at FEM, and the FEM family.

Chapter Four

TRANSITION AND LIFE AFTER THE BANK

Irene Mureithi

I had started preparing myself to transition from employment into entrepreneurship even before my life-changing Hilton session. In 2006, I took a US$3,000 loan from the Savings and Credit Cooperative Society (Sacco) run by my employer, and registered for an online entrepreneurship class.

I took an entrepreneurship and real estate course offered by Trump University (also known as the Trump Wealth Institute and Trump Entrepreneur Initiative LLC) which was an American company that ran a real estate training program from 2005 to 2010.[4] People warned me saying it was a scam but what I learned from the course was quite valuable, and is tangible for me to this date.

The thoughts of owning real estate were planted in my mind as I took that course. In 2007,

I received a prophetic word from Evangelist Wairimu about a real estate venture. It was surprising having completed a secular training on real estate the previous year. Today I am involved in developing Serian Country Homes in Naivasha, Nakuru County. I invited a few friends who are now shareholders and together we own 20 acres of land. On 30th September 2023, we had a groundbreaking ceremony. We are developing phase one which is 44 housing units and later on, phase two with a similar number. We thank God for the breathtaking views of Mount Longonot and a complete aerial view of Lake Naivasha. When complete, these will be beautiful retirement and holiday homes.

The reason I share this story is to encourage and at the same time caution the readers on the power of the mind. It is a fertile garden. Whatever seed – you sow by exposing yourself to information – through audio, visual, and written means, networking – whether good or bad – will ultimately germinate and grow. As we all know, in a garden there are weeds and flowers. You also need to be careful who you allow to speak into your life. The choice is yours! Make a great one.

The Hilton session clarified that I am a people person, and I am gifted with the ability to inspire others. I believe it's not just my personality style. It is the gift of God in me. After the Hilton, I began to focus on getting more information on what I could do based on my DISC report. I came across more information that linked possible career choices with one's personality style. Coaching was listed under the category of my style and that's what got me thinking about a coaching business as an expression of my purpose. Then I talked to Dr. Stanko about becoming a certified behavioral analyst. I took the program, passed the exam, and became a certified behavioral analyst using the DISC assessment. The more I thought about coaching, the more I was convinced it would lead me to the fulfillment of my purpose.

In the midst of all these things, I was thinking of how to pay my mortgage so I would be free to resign from the bank. I had seen other colleagues leave the bank with their mortgages, but when they were unable to pay, it was stressful because the bank still needed the loan to be repaid in full. I didn't want that kind of shame and stress. To cut a long story short, I made a proposal to one of my managers in the bank and she took over the mortgage and bought the house. It is still hers to this day. I was then free to leave the bank debt free. Of course, that didn't sit well with my family. They thought I was making a huge mistake at a young age. It seemed like I had no future in terms of a career and was careening towards poverty.

The low-hanging fruit towards fulfilling my purpose was corporate training because I knew establishing a coaching business would take some time. However, I had no guarantees on which organizations would open their doors to me. Purpose is an ongoing process. You have to embrace the uncertainties. Maybe this is why people are afraid to take the risks to move from their comfort zones to the purpose zone.

As you read, I'm sure you are looking for helpful tips so you can discover your purpose. We

have alluded to some, which I have summarized below, with more to come.
1. Ask yourself powerful questions (Who am I? Why am I here? If I had all the money what would I do to positively impact society?).
2. Get a coach and invest in a coaching program.
3. Clarify your personality style through various assessments (DISC is highly recommended).
4. Pray and search the Word for the leading of the Holy Spirit (this is the most important one).

You have to embrace the purpose journey, or as Dr. Stanko calls it, your PurposeQuest. A driver can't see the whole road as (s)he heads towards their destination, but (s)he can use the headlights to see the next 106 meters. I believe that is how God leads. He doesn't show us the whole route, just the next steps in front of us. It's really a journey of faith.

November 1, 2007 birthed a new season in my life. I finally left the bank. I embraced my life purpose and I have never looked back, either in the storms or the sunshine. As I write, I am celebrating 16 years of God's faithfulness, grace, provision, protection, joy, peace and all the trials that come with a purpose-driven life.

What a beautiful time to be writing this book! I'm a November baby so I get to celebrate my birthday and my purpose 'birth' in the same month. Isn't it interesting that the Word of God says in Jeremiah 1:5, "Before I formed you in the womb I knew you [and approved of you as My chosen instrument], And before you were born I consecrated you [to Myself as My own]; I have appointed you as a prophet to the nations." November is my favorite month for obvious reasons!

As I continued to read and reflect on the results of my profile and coaching session, it not only gave me insight into who I am but also insight into other people and their styles. When I would talk to some of my colleagues and hint that I wanted to transition, I could see the fear on their faces on my behalf. Once I had done the profile, I knew that they did not share my profile style. The profile helped me understand that all people process information and opportunities differently.

They were trying to understand what I was saying but they couldn't see the future as I could. Some were genuinely empathetic as they thought this was the worst career decision one could make at the age of 33. Others didn't care much. After all, "your career, your choice." Everyone is busy with their own life and the cares that come with it.

This said, do we stop to think that God has invested so much in us from before we were born, and that we will give an account when we stand before Him? Life cannot be lived just from our own choices. We have to choose to align with God's big picture for our lives with eternity in mind.

As the Bible says in Ecclesiastes 3:11, "He has made everything beautiful and appropriate in its time. He has also planted eternity [a sense of divine *purpose*] (emphasis added) in the human heart [a mysterious longing which nothing under the sun can satisfy, except God]—yet man cannot find out (comprehend, grasp) what God has done (His overall plan) from the beginning to the end."

My loving mother is an 'S' style (in the DISC) and formally worked in only two organizations until her retirement in her late 50s. She couldn't fathom how I held a bank job for only 10 years and resigned from it in my early 30s. She, on the other hand, is as steady as they come. Mom held one job for six years and the other for 25 years. Before her formal employment, she had several odd jobs to make ends meet as a single mum. Those who have followed me on social media for some time know that I spare nothing in taking care of Mom and Grandmother. They sacrificed the best they had in their days to raise my siblings and me. It's an honor to love and care for them in their retirement.

I always encourage my friends and online followers to do the same for those who are privileged to still have their parents alive. It doesn't have to be expensive. Whatever is given out of love holds the most value. One of the narratives I have constantly challenged in Kenya is how we wait until people die to pour tributes and money towards their funerals. We call it RIP (Rest In Peace) but one of my friends, John Mbindyo, taught me a concept called KIP (Keep In Peace) – give people their flowers while they are still alive and can enjoy their scent and beauty.

For Mum, my career transition was a terrifying thing. For me, there was fear but there was also excitement when I thought of all the possibilities. As I mentioned before, different personality styles process information differently. This is one of the reasons there are conflicts in families, workplaces, churches, and social groups, even when people mean well for each other. Over time, I came to see why Dr. Stanko and I work so well together, and this is because we are two different styles who understand each other's profiles. I understand his personality and he understands mine. The DISC really was, and continues to be, a game changer for me and hundreds of other clients I have exposed to the profile. I have seen it work wonders for corporate colleagues, couples, teens, and even children.

After I left the bank, I started engaging in corporate training in January 2008. I mostly trained banks and insurance companies on things like communication, emotional intelligence, conflict resolution, change management, and leadership. We also conducted DISC assessment for some of the organizations. I was finally happy doing work I enjoyed. However, the joy was short-lived as Kenya continued to experience post-election violence between 2007 and 2008. Some organizations cut back on their corporate training budgets due to political uncertainty. This affected my newly-found stream of income.

When this happened, I went through a baptism by fire as my new source of income (corporate training) dried up. No sooner had I started my purpose journey than financial challenges set in. Remember the mortgaged house I sold so I could resign from the bank? When I did this, I started renting a different house in the same estate. When the corporate jobs dried up, things were so tough that I couldn't even pay the rent.

My landlady kicked me out and I became homeless within the estate.

I ended up being housed by one of my former bank colleagues, the late Shenan Kamotho, a very kind woman who chose not to judge me and instead welcomed me and two other people who lived with me at that time. Some of my colleagues who knew of my predicament used to laugh until the cows came home. They would say I resigned without a plan. Some asked whether pursuing purpose can pay bills. I don't blame them. Living a life of purpose has an element of sacrifice. Jesus is our perfect example. The cross was painful, yet it was not the end. It was just a season.

As we encourage you to pursue your life purpose, please note that we are not promising you a life without challenges. In fact, there will be many challenges. For some like me, it was financial. For others, it will be something different. We see the same for people in the Bible who pursued their purpose, like the Apostle Paul. We also see it in modern day heroes who continue to live out a life of purpose.

Allow the Scripture below from Philippians 2:8-11 to encourage you:

> After He was found in [terms of His] outward appearance as a man [for a divinely-appointed time], He humbled Himself [still further] by becoming obedient [to the Father] to the point of death, even death on a cross. For this reason also [because He obeyed and so completely humbled Himself], God has highly exalted Him and bestowed on Him the name

which is above every name, so that at the name of Jesus every knee shall bow [in submission], of those who are in heaven and on earth and under the earth, and that every tongue will confess and openly acknowledge that Jesus Christ is Lord (sovereign God), to the glory of God the Father.

Think about Apostle Paul and his path to purpose. Bible readers are familiar with his Damascus journey and transition from Saul to Paul. In many of the epistles, some of which he wrote while in jail (purpose), he demystified some of the erroneous teachings that only promise bliss when people are in pursuit of their purpose. Divine purpose has both joys and intense pain. In Philippians 4:11-13, Paul says:

> Not that I speak from [any personal] need, for I have learned to be content [and self-sufficient through Christ, satisfied to the point where I am not disturbed or uneasy] regardless of my circumstances. I know how to get along and live humbly [in difficult times], and I also know how to enjoy abundance and live in prosperity. In any and every circumstance I have learned the secret [of facing life], whether well-fed or going hungry, whether having an abundance or being in need. I can do all things [which He has called me to do] through Him who strengthens and empowers me [to fulfill His *purpose*—I am self-sufficient in Christ's sufficiency; I am ready for anything and equal to anything

through Him who infuses me with inner strength and confident peace.] (emphasis added).

When Shenan took me in with my two family members, other friends within the estate had to store different household items for me in their homes. Some stored our beds, while others kept the sofa set and kitchen items. I was homeless, just not on the streets. To this day, some of my family and close friends can't understand why I put myself through "unnecessary trouble." I didn't plan to be homeless or a bother to people. I am eternally grateful that God has changed the season of homelessness and given me a home – a divine provision I will mention later.

So, there's a price to pay. The greater the scope of the assignment, the greater the price and prize. Dr. Stanko refers to the financial difficulties we encounter in our pursuit of purpose as "financial terrorism." He says, "If the enemy of our souls can't keep us from purpose, he will try to starve us out so we will quit." I can take you back to the spot when Dr. Stanko said these words to me. We were riding in a taxi (cab) near the Kenya Wildlife Service (KWS) gate on Lang'ata Road.

The KWS is mandated to conserve and protect Kenya's wildlife. In an eerie twist, that spot is also right opposite Nairobi's public cemetery. In this season of my life, I was experiencing financial terrorism. It seemed like the death of my purpose journey. It felt like the end of the road. Thoughts of throwing in the towel consumed my heart and mind. I was literally straddling a paradox.

I had two options: to conserve and protect

my purpose, or to bury it. Thank God He sent me my purpose coach just in time. He not only encouraged me to stay the course, but he also gave me US$1,000 before he left the country to help me take care of my immediate bills. The power of divine connections is something that should never be taken for granted.

I didn't quit. I'm glad I didn't.

I think the lives that God has impacted and continues to impact through my purpose journey are the greatest reward I can receive on this side of eternity. I envision the Master saying, "Well done, good and faithful servant. You have been faithful and trustworthy over a little, I will put you in charge of many things; ... share in the joy of your master" (Matthew 25:21, 23).

While I was conducting corporate trainings in 2008 and 2009, I noticed a certain dynamic during our tea times. At ten o'clock or four o'clock tea or during lunch, people were interested in my personal story about resigning from the bank. In retrospect, they too were probably bored beyond belief but couldn't verbalize their frustrations as they were still in their comfort zone.

They probably admired the courage and freedom I was experiencing. Over the years, some of my friends in the corporate world have taken a risk and whispered in my ears of their desperate need for freedom. If only they could figure a way to pay their bills, some would have resigned the next day. However, I also have friends who truly enjoy what they do in the corporate world. These ones don't experience "Monday Blues." They are driven by "Monday Motivation."

As a coach, I've come across many people working for organizations who have no joy in their jobs. They spend their days fantasizing about an exit strategy. Unfortunately, some overstay their comfort zones and end up being rendered redundant.

The more I thought about the people I was interacting with during the corporate trainings, the more I could see the gap between professional development and personal development. This fueled a desire in me to provide a platform where professionals and entrepreneurs would come for their personal development needs. It had to be a safe space for conversations that are difficult to have in the corporate setting.

On April 7, 2010, we launched the Personal Development Institute (PDI). Voila! Finally there was a platform where people could come from different corporations, and we could have conversations about their life purpose while still working in the corporate world. This continues to the present day. We have trained thousands of people in the last 13 years. Their purpose journey and their impact in the community are stories for another book.

My PDI co-founder, Dr. Emma Karari, a renowned Kenyan cardiologist, was the first person who believed in the PDI vision and invested her money to help me get the dream off the ground. We opened our doors to 20 students at 6 p.m. on April 7, 2010. We were housed at CITAM Valley Road where the church had sublet us a small space to run morning and evening in-person classes.

The flagship program at PDI was and is still called Transformed and Renewed Mind (TRM). We cover several modules in TRM:

YOUR PURPOSE JOURNEY

1. Spiritual intelligence: We cover one's purpose in detail, and also talk about rediscovering the Kingdom of God.
2. Emotional intelligence: Today much of the world knows the value of emotional intelligence, a must-have skill. We cover the five components of EI, but what makes the module outstanding are the practical case studies.
3. Social intelligence: We are social beings and are made to connect. We take an in-depth look at all relationships in this module.
4. Health and wellness: This is facilitated by medical doctors and nutritionists. It's all about our wellness – including emotional health.
5. Financial intelligence: We all need to improve our money management habits to create generational wealth.
6. Leadership and strategic planning: As the CEO of your life, you are in charge of your daily decisions. Do you have a strategic plan?
7. Careers and entrepreneurship: We talk about professional development as well as build skills in intra/entrepreneurship.
8. Self-Awareness: We use DISC and other assessments to offer practical knowledge of oneself.
9. Fun and recreation: Work without

play makes Jack a dull boy. We organize recreational trips and combine them with mind shift moments. We have different facilitators who teach various modules based on the concept of the Wheel of Life. Purpose doesn't exist in a vacuum. It is carried out in the midst of family, career, finances, and all the other aspects that make up life, hence all the different modules that we teach. We have captured all this in great detail in a book titled, *The Secret Brilliance*. I co-authored this with other PDI alumni, and it's available in both soft and hard copies.

While running the PDI programs, I made the move to Karen. We rented a business premise which was on Karen Lane off Karen Road, a leafy suburb in Nairobi. Three years later after we had moved, it became financially unsustainable. To be honest, I consider this a business mistake I made as a young entrepreneur. Due to high recurrent expenditure and a decline in the number of students, we slowly found ourselves in the red, with a debt of about US$20,000.

It took my mentor, the late Dr. James Mageria, the then chairman of Karen Hospital, to bail me out. He believed in me, and I will forever treasure his words, "My beloved daughter, Irene, as a seasoned businessman I cannot allow a banana peel on the marathon track to keep you from the race. It's an honor to help you and at the same time to teach you how to do Kingdom business more effectively."

With that investment, we cleared the rent debt and moved out of Karen. Talk about repositioning oneself. It was such a transition. It was during that season when I shared a cab with Dr. Stanko and he talked to me about what he called economic terrorism, which I mentioned earlier.

You see now it's been a journey. I'm still learning, unlearning and relearning, and I thank God for the "never say die" spirit. The impact the program has made in the lives of many people is tangible and measurable. As a result of the feedback received over the years, the value and the price of the PDI programs have also gone up. We now run customized online classes and offer more handholding on how to clarify and monetize one's life purpose. It is very personalized coaching.

Chapter Five
MY PURPOSE STORY
John Stanko

As Irene and I were working on this manuscript, I was intrigued by her purpose story and journey – some of which I knew and, believe it or not, some I was learning for the first time. I thought, *That's what I should do. I will include my own purpose story alongside hers*. Therefore, I went into my books and articles on purpose to find something I could copy and paste for this chapter, for surely it existed somewhere in the volumes I have written.

Alas, I was mistaken and that was quite a surprise to me. While I have told my story hundreds of times and have written parts of the story in many places, I could not find my entire story in one place. That isn't right, so I am going to correct that error right here and now by telling you my purpose story from the beginning, which for me was 1991 (I know I said I was not going to get into ancient history, but please indulge me just this once. I won't do it again).

YOUR PURPOSE JOURNEY

In 1991, my pastor came to me with a group of men who had an idea for a business that involved selling advertising for an attachment that went under a landline phone (I told you this was ancient history; who has a landline phone these days?). Since I had a master's degree in economics, they asked me to lead the business team, promising me a $30,000 salary once things got rolling—which I was assured was just a matter of time.

That was all I needed to move into high gear. We signed a lease for office space and a phone, got office equipment and furniture, and hired on a few more salespeople. We had meetings where we established a business plan (complete with Bible verses, I might add), and prayed elaborate prayers with eyes closed and hands held, signs of our earnestness and fervor. When we dedicated the office to God's glory, a pastor came and heaved globs of anointing oil all over the place when he prayed, and we didn't clean off the walls. The oil that slowly moved its way down the walls was only a visible symbol of our certain anointing.

There was only one problem: through all our efforts and my organizational skills, God never got the message we were even in business. In nine months, we were out of money and had only a few prospects signed up for the service. All those people who formed a circle and held hands to fervently pray began to jump ship, and before I knew it, I was the only one left to try and salvage the business. To make matters worse, my name was on all the leases (we did not have time to incorporate, so as the team leader, I used my signature to guarantee payment).

The Bible says when we pray, we should go find a quiet place, and I certainly felt led to pray because I was left holding the bag for a lot of lease payments. The quietest place I knew of was our business office (the phones never rang and no one ever came by), so I went one morning to ask, rather to plead with God to save the business. As I sat behind my desk, I raised my hands in prayer (not real high, just shoulder high), closed my eyes, and prayed this prayer, "Oh Lord, save this business for Your glory!" When I got to the word glory, I needed something special, something that would give the prayer more pizazz when it reached God's ears. That's when I thought of a woman we had called the glory lady.

This woman was in the first church I attended after I came to the Lord. She sat in the last row and had hair stacked up on top of her head. When she liked something going on in church – a prayer, a message, an exhortation – she would say "Glory!" but she said it with a voice lower than the Dead Sea with the same amount of vibrato every time: "Gloooooorrrrryyyyy!" On that morning in my office, my prayer needed a boost so I copied the Glory Lady's style and said, "Lord, save this business for your Gloooooorrrrryyyyy." I thought I had done well.

As soon as my prayer was finished, this thought came running through my mind: *You're not interested in God's glory; you just want to save your own neck.* That was true. I was praying a religious prayer because I thought it would work best, but if I would have been truthful, I was angry and upset that God was not helping me in this business endeavor. I had done everything I knew to do and we had ended in failure, and I was not a happy man.

I opened my eyes, lowered my hands, and pounded my desk, shouting, "If You didn't create me to start this business, what did you create me to do?" Keep in mind, I wasn't looking for information; I was simply venting my anger toward God.

To my surprise, my mind immediately went to Genesis 1:2. I wasn't thinking Bible, I hadn't been reading Genesis, and I wasn't in the mood for a Bible study. Yet I had no choice but to go to Genesis, since the impression was so strong, and there I read, "Now the earth was formless and empty, darkness was over the surface of the deep, and the Spirit of God was hovering over the waters." Don't ask me why, but I had a Bible commentary in the office and I got it off the shelf to read what it had to say about this verse, the commentary had this to say: "The Spirit was there to bring order out of chaos."

Order out of chaos.

That morning, in the midst of my confusion and anger, I realized I had found my life's purpose. All throughout my young life (I was 31 at the time) I had loved to organize. As an eight-year-old, I would empty my father's garage, clean it out, hose it down, and put everything back. When I was done, I would stand in the middle of the garage and have this inexplicable sense of peace and joy. I would replicate that experience wherever I was: set things in order that were out of order and then have a sense of accomplishment.

I didn't know what to do with what I learned that morning after my "Gloooooooorrrrryyyyy" prayer, so I didn't do anything. I reflected, read, and studied what "order out of chaos" meant and concluded that I had indeed found my purpose. I also assumed if I had a purpose, then others did too, but I didn't know the implications for that in my life—until I moved to Orlando, Florida in 1989 to pastor a church. In addition to the church, I led a prison ministry that met weekly with a discipleship group of inmates.

I decided to experiment with a purpose message I had developed with my prison discipleship group. The men were intrigued and we had some great, insightful discussions. I also shared some of the concepts with my small home group in Orlando, and I saw the makings of a nice message on finding purpose.

It was then that I was invited to help my friends at Integrity Music develop a worship weekend seminar. We agreed that I should teach something on leadership while I was there, so I premiered a message titled "Effectiveness: Finding Your Life Purpose." The rest is history as I have gone on to deliver that message more than 1,000 times in many countries, including sessions all across Kenya and through media outlets with Irene.

What are the lessons from my purpose story that can and will help you with your purpose? Let's look at a few:

1. Your purpose is summarized in one simple statement that has profound meaning for your life only. It is usually

accompanied by a verse or passage from the Bible that depicts what the statement means.
2. Most people don't know their purpose because they don't ask and keep on asking.
3. Sometimes we don't ask because we don't really believe we will receive an answer. If I found an answer and I wasn't even looking for one, how much more will you find an answer from God if you seek with honest, faith-filled intent?
4. Once people find purpose, they often want to know what to do. I didn't do anything, but instead spent time (years actually) meditating on what I heard and praying about what it meant. God wants you to know and fulfill your purpose more than you. You are not alone, and God will help you all along the way to know what to do once you know who you are.
5. Many people want to know how their purpose will translate into income because they start to think how their purpose will express itself. My advice is for them to focus on what it is they are supposed to do and not think about money, which only complicates and discourages the process of finding purpose.
6. Once you find purpose, you will often

be called upon by others to help them find theirs.

I have shared that story many times in various nations, and it never gets old. In fact, it refreshes and encourages me every time I tell or write it. The purpose message brought me to Kenya and my work there remains the most sacred and special of all my purpose outreach ministry. It represents something God did for me in that I did not work to introduce the message there. I came at the invitation of a woman I had never met and before I knew it, the purpose message had invaded the hearts and minds of the Kenyan people.

I still marvel at the door God opened for me in Kenya and there is no end in sight – or at least, I hope there isn't. I have developed and introduced much of my purpose material in Kenya simply because I have talked about it there so often. The same is true for the personality profiles I have used extensively in my coaching in Kenya, which we will discuss in a later chapter. For now, let's get back to Irene and her purpose journey.

Chapter Six
THE LEAN YEARS

Irene Mureithi

I had so much to learn about business as you have already seen by the stories I have told. In my early years, I skimmed through details which is quite natural for someone with an optimistic style. Today, however, I am very keen on details, and I achieve this by collaborating with people whose natural strength lies in reading and analyzing the fine print. I go to great lengths to ensure that we have looked and relooked at the bottom line.

When we moved to the Karen location, I had assumed PDI would continue to grow, and thus we expanded based on that assumption. Sometimes things were very tight and I would be the last person to receive a salary, which wasn't even that much to talk about. It was a season where I felt very alone and misunderstood although I was surrounded by well-meaning, supportive and successful people.

It reminded me of a story Dr. Stanko told me of an elderly banker who was approached by his successor who asked him, "Sir, can you please give me a clue or secret to your longevity and success?"

The old man answered, "I made good decisions."

The younger man responded, "That's great, but how do I get to that point in my career that I too can make good decisions?"

The old man said, "You need experience."

The young man was becoming frustrated with the old man's curt answers, but he decided to press in with one more question: "So sir, how can I get this needed experience?"

And the old man's final answer was, "By making bad decisions!"

I made some bad decisions along the way that were due to my inexperience and total trust in some who seemed to know what they were advising me to do. In the end, I paid a high price for those "bad decisions," and I trust they have equipped me to make better decisions going forward.

When times were tough, I occasionally questioned whether I was in the perfect will of God. I asked God some questions about my motives and if I had made the right decision. However, at no point did I think about going out to get a job. At my lowest point, I was just hoping someone would call and give me US$200 so I could meet the day's obligations. However, God is faithful, and I did get a call one day and someone gave me US$80,000, enough to buy another house in cash, which I did. This gift came at the lowest point of my life after I had moved out from Karen and had suffered a total burnout.

What a surprise blessing, and one of the joys of pursuing purpose in and out of season. Walking with God is not a walk in the park. We see this even in the life of Abraham, the father of faith. It can sometimes be difficult, and your thoughts can range from great faith to deep fear and doubt. Yet when those blessings come and you know it was God who gave them, it's an occasion for profound thanksgiving and praise. No wonder Sarah called their promised son, Isaac, which means laughter.

Psalm 126:1-3 has come alive as I've watched God restore my life and business in the recent past:

> When the Lord brought back the captives to Zion (Jerusalem), we were like those who dream [it seemed so unreal. Then our mouth was filled with laughter and our tongue with joyful shouting; Then they said among the nations, "The Lord has done great things for them." The Lord has done great things for us; We are glad!

The divine provision to purchase a house meant I would never be homeless again. Yet, we can all take comfort in the story of Abraham. Even though God had given him the land on which he walked, he had to leave that land twice due to famine and drought. When God promises to give us something, He will test us. He tested me.

Remember Shenan Kamotho, the kind lady who hosted me when I was homeless? One day she invited a friend who would later turn out to be my new landlady. I consider her a gift from God to this day. She was very understanding and would say, "Irene, I perceive you're a woman of God and I can see what you're trying to do. We are going to support you. Even if you don't pay the house rent on the fifth, [which is the date most Kenyans pay house rent], as long as you pay on any date within the month, it will be fine."

With that assurance, I moved out of Shenan's house where we had been housed for three months into Betty Abuto Ouma's apartment. Betty and her family were relocating to London where they live to this day, and she allowed me into her house without a deposit.

She would often call me from the UK to check on me and pray with me even when I had not paid her rent. When I would get into arrears, she would tell me not to worry, and that she was confident I would pay once I got the money, which I did. Her words on the phone were a constant encouragement: "From my house, you'll go into your own house," which is exactly what happened.

What made it more miraculous was that my landlady, Betty, was not from my tribe. The landlady who kicked me out and rendered me homeless was from my tribe. And this is why I tell my fellow Kenyans to never put their hope on tribal alliances, but instead, deal with each person on a heart-to-heart basis.

Betty was, and is still, deeply Kingdom-minded. She was able to support me even though I was not from her tribe. And I have been to others what she was to me – a godsend in my time of need.

Proverbs 18:24(b) says, "But there is a [true, loving] friend who [is reliable and] sticks closer than a brother." This is who Betty has been in my life since we met. Her family is very special to me.

As you can tell, it's been a process over a span of time. I want you to understand that when I had to leave Karen, there was no immediate provision or breakthrough. Eventually, God provided the US$80,000, but up to that time, I was thinking, *Here I go again. Lord, what will people think of me?*

If you would ask what is the one lesson I learned after my departure from Karen, it's this: keep recurrent expenditure as low as possible. Later, I did get an office on Ngong Road under the banner of Kingdom Business Network and I worked from there for a couple of years until Covid-19 hit. We all had to work from home and it's in that season when I transitioned all our PDI programs online, enabling us to serve more people in many countries.

And another important lesson I learnt in my difficult financial years was not to trust people as much as I did. Even when people are attracted to your vision, they don't exactly see it the way you do. Some don't see it from an eternal perspective of purpose. They see it purely as a business, and when the return on investment does not make sense to them, they may walk out on you.

For the person like me who is a visionary, it's more than a business. It's a calling. It's my divine assignment. Even when the return on investment financially is not making sense, I stick to it. I know Dr. Stanko is well acquainted with the purpose journey, as are many other people who live a Kingdom, purpose-driven life. Money is not the primary motivation. It's mission first, money second.

The third lesson is that when people leave your vision, it is part of the process, so I had to learn to release people. The fourth lesson I learned is how the various personality styles of the DISC profile play out in real life – and it is a fascinating study. For example, when I look back at some of the people I have worked with, I realized they were more of a 'C' style. As much as they loved me as a person, it was the facts and figures that were not making sense for them. Therefore, they made a decision to walk away. From their personality and their perspective, there was no need to stay plugged into the vision.

Chapter Seven
PURPOSE INSIGHTS
Irene Mureithi

Finally, let me speak to the matter of my relationship with Dr. Stanko as a coach. God has been my source of strength through it all, but the other thing that gave me staying power is my relationship with him. Thankfully, he would come to Kenya almost every year and we would get to hang out. I would share my challenges and he would always encourage me. He gave me most of his books. There is that stability of my purpose coach working with me throughout the years that sustained me. He kept me focused on my purpose. For that, I will be forever grateful and will honor him every chance I have.

I firmly believe what the Bible says, that "before I formed you in your mother's womb, I knew you" (Jeremiah 1:5). That was Jeremiah's call to purpose and I maintain, as Dr. Stanko does, that every one of us has a purpose just like Jeremiah's. It's clear and simple but it's profound and merits us giving our lives to fulfill it. The truth of personality undergirds our purpose. There's a way you are assigned to fulfill your purpose that is consistent with your personality. Dr. Stanko and I both teach the purpose message, but we do so in alignment to who we are in Christ.

Our personality styles vary greatly, and this means that we deliver the same message differently. We want you to be you in your purpose journey. You can learn from others like I have learned from Dr. Stanko and my other coaches and mentors – but be consistent with who God made you to be. Be your authentic self. Don't be a copy of anyone else, including the people you admire. You are unique and therefore, the expression of your purpose will be unique too.

I lean more on exhortation and inspiration expressed through speech. Dr. Stanko's message is consistent with the 'C' style and thus he has written over 80 books and actually keeps count of how many people he's met with! This is in line with his preference for detail-orientation in DISC.

The purpose message is still, after all is said and done, the core of all that I do. I know that even in purpose, people operate differently because of their various personality styles. Since 2007, the message has grown and matured, and I have incorporated other things to clarify the message. I am careful not to encourage people to run off in pursuit of purpose without paying attention to family responsibilities and their financial needs.

Anyone pursuing purpose has to be prepared that not everyone is going to understand your journey. My family didn't. Initially, my mom thought I had lost my mind when I shared with her that I was planning to resign from the bank. Other relatives have over the years said I made a bad career move. They say things like, "If you had stayed in the bank, you'd be a big shot within the banking industry." For me, the response is always, "What is the point of having lots of money and being unhappy?"

My priority in life is to do the work of Him who sent me here. Again, Jesus is my perfect example. We see in Scripture His perspective of food and that of His disciples differed. Does this mean Jesus did not eat? Certainly not! He has the divine formula of increasing fish and bread and turning water into wine. He also cursed the fig tree for not having fruit. In John 4:31-34, Jesus spelt out that His real food (what mattered most to Him) was to fulfill His divine assignment.

> Meanwhile, the disciples were urging Jesus [to have a meal], saying, "Rabbi (Teacher), eat." But He told them, "I have food to eat that you do not know about." So the disciples said to one another, "Has anyone brought Him something to eat?" Jesus said to them, "My food is to do the will of Him who sent Me and to completely finish His work."

I am a believer in abundance. I'm the visionary of TKC Business, a Kingdom business and investment club that has raised and invested US$800,000 in the last six months (May – October 2023) through our strategic partnership with Nabo Capital. By the time this book goes to print, we most likely will have raised US$1 million on our way to our goal of US$10 million and beyond. Our vision is to create generational wealth so that the children of God can pursue their divine purpose without the challenges that come with poverty. As you have read in the previous chapters, I made many money mistakes. I believe God was training me in the same way David was trained in the wilderness for the palace.

In Scripture, we see God raising Joseph from the pit to the palace, and Ruth from collecting the leftovers of grain in the field to owning the land. These are all examples of purpose-driven people. God is more interested in making us and then finally entrusting us with the resources we need to fulfill our divine assignment. When you put money before mission, it never ends well. The opposite is true. When mission (purpose) consumes your heart and you remain faithful with or without money, in the end God gives you the money too.

In a previous chapter, I highlighted some of the modules we teach at PDI. You now see why we teach financial intelligence, social intelligence, and emotional intelligence, among others. Purpose is multifaceted. Our family and other relationships in the marketplace matter. Our health is important because we cannot fulfill purpose on a sick bed. Financial struggles will make one give up on purpose.

We need a holistic approach to the subject of purpose. Rest and relaxation are important in this journey. Even Jesus withdrew from the masses and His disciples to get rest, pray, and connect with His Father. Our Father in heaven is the sole giver of all divine assignments. When did you last spend time with Him?

PDI has partnered with several churches in Kenya to promote the purpose message. Some churches have been kind enough to offer their platforms for us to not only share the purpose message, but also run various PDI programs for their members on Sunday afternoons after service. We thank the church leadership of various congregations in Kenya and beyond for their partnership.

For people who have heard over and over again that they have a purpose, but can't identify it for various reasons, PDI exists to help you. This is why we have the year-in, year-out purpose classes and seminars to help people discover their purpose when they are ready to do so.

There are thousands of people who have clarified their life's purpose through our programs and are doing significant Kingdom exploits in the marketplace. Now that we have recently launched the PDI-TKC Media, we shall be hosting them on the show to share their purpose journey. This will encourage many people to realize that it's possible to clarify and live out their purpose. If you're reading this book and you're new to PDI-TKC, we encourage you to follow us on social media and stay updated.

The challenge I find among some church people is that they tend to be more religious in their thinking than they are Kingdom-minded. Since purpose is really a Kingdom issue, the interest in finding and fulfilling purpose isn't always there if they're not inclined to a Kingdom mindset.

You've got to understand who you are in the Kingdom of God to appreciate that you have a unique purpose, one assigned to you by the King of the Kingdom. You then know what God expects from you and only you to fulfill your purpose. This is why in 2021 PDI developed a new program called The Kingdom Connect (TKC) to help people understand who they are in the Kingdom of God and how Kingdom principles work in the marketplace.

TKC has grown in the last three years from a membership of 38 people and is now serving over 1,000 people consistently through social media, Sunday evening classes, Tuesday evening business classes, etc. We are a global online platform for Kingdom minded professionals and entrepreneurs in various nations.

It's important to see Jesus living out His life purpose as a king. It helps you to understand that you too are a king and a priest in the Kingdom. The Kingdom sets you free from a religious mentality where people can tend to think everybody is called to work in the church.

Jesus' work had Him spend more time in the marketplace than He did in the synagogues of His day. Therefore, the purpose of many of His followers may also be in the marketplace and not necessarily at the pulpit – although there is certainly nothing wrong with serving in the Church. However, the Kingdom sets you free from feeling as though the ministers in the pulpit are more anointed than you. We are all anointed by the same Holy Spirit. Some are anointed for the marketplace and others for the pulpit.

This understanding will set you free. We see many case studies in Scripture where God would appoint and anoint people for tasks like craftsmanship. In Kenya we would say *kazi ya mjengo* (construction work). We mistakenly tend to think that the person at the pulpit is more anointed than the construction worker. Reading the Scripture below paints a different picture. Every child of God who has the Holy Spirit is appointed and anointed for their divine assignment.

> Then the Lord spoke to Moses, saying: "See, I have called by name Bezalel the son of Uri, the son of Hur, of the tribe of Judah. And I have filled him with the Spirit of God, in wisdom, in understanding, in knowledge, and in all manner of workmanship, to design artistic works, to work in gold, in silver, in bronze, in cutting jewels for setting, in carving wood, and to work in all manner of workmanship. "And I, indeed I, have appointed with him Aholiab the son of Ahisamach, of the tribe of Dan; and I have put wisdom in the hearts of all the gifted artisans, that they may make all that I have commanded you" (Exodus 31:1-6, NKJV).

Maybe your purpose is to be a beautician. Some people think there's no anointing on that, but think about Esther in the Bible. Her story is amazing. We can draw coaching, mentorship, and training principles from this story. The narrative takes place in a palace, not a church. Although the name of God is not directly mentioned in the book of Esther, each chapter is filled with divine clues of the unseen hand of God orchestrating her promotion. It's important to note that this promotion was for the deliverance of a nation. Purpose is never about you. It's always about others.

Hegai was very impressed with Esther and treated her kindly. He quickly ordered a special menu for her and provided her with beauty treatments (Esther 2:9, NLT).

Maybe your purpose is to be a government official. Some people think if you are working in government, there's no anointing needed for leadership. On the contrary, both in the Old and New Testaments, we see the anointing of God resting upon kings, prophets, priests, and people who served God in what today we call the marketplace. In Acts 10:1-4, we read,

> Now at Caesarea [Maritima] there was a man named Cornelius, a centurion of what was known as the Italian Regiment, a devout man and one who, along with all his household, feared God. He made many charitable donations to the Jewish people, and prayed to God always. About the ninth hour (3:00 p.m.) of the day he clearly saw in a vision an angel of God who had come to him and said, "Cornelius!" Cornelius was frightened and stared intently at him and said, "What is it, lord (sir)?" And the angel said to him, "Your prayers and gifts of charity have ascended as a memorial offering before God [an offering made in remembrance of His past blessings]."

The message of the Kingdom of God helps to renew your mind. You become transformed and begin to evaluate everything through your relationship with your King and the domain where He has assigned you. It's a wonderful way to live and serve God. While many may talk about the Kingdom, some don't fully embrace the message because it's radical. It sets people free from their limitations and from small thinking.

The same thing happens through the message of purpose. People get set free in such a way that even when they exercise leadership, it's from a place of servanthood as opposed to lording it over the people. Jesus was and remains the greatest servant leader.

When you find purpose, you have found your mandate from headquarters – your heavenly headquarters. You don't need anybody's permission. You don't need anybody's approval. The King, the head of the Kingdom, has told you what He wants, and where He wants you to express it. He gives you the gifts that will help you fulfill that purpose. You will need to collaborate with other people in their purpose because this is God's design. The late Dr. Myles Munroe was a great purpose teacher. He used to say, "Orange trees do not eat their own oranges." Instead of competition, we need to embrace strategic partnerships that will help every person and organization thrive in their purpose.

We've really turned the meaning of Ephesians 4:11-12 around. Instead of equipping the saints for the work of ministry, we are equipping the ministry to exist and thrive through the work of the saints. Unfortunately, this leads to frustration in the long run for people with a religious mindset. They think, "I'm doing what's required of me. I go to church. I serve in my church, and then I go home and take care of my family. I go to work. I eat, and eventually, I'm going to die." We should be telling people there's a whole lot more to life besides these things.

Sometimes I see frustrated believers who are angry with the Church. You see how they express that anger even on social media. There is a part of me that says, "You as a believer have the Holy Spirit. You have a responsibility to find your purpose. You can't entirely blame the church leadership or the church if you've not found your purpose. You don't need anyone's permission to be purposeful. It's *your* purpose, not the church's or the congregation's. You must take responsibility for every facet of your life! You cannot derive your joy, peace, prosperity from a company or a church." These are hard truths, but the truth will set us free! (John 8:32).

We have all been hurt in the family, at work or church. Finding healing is important. When we don't heal, we saddle ourselves with the baggage of bitterness. When this continues for long, we end up wasting our professional and personal potential. Our gifts in ministry are sacrificed at the altar of pity-parties instead of becoming a living sacrifice acceptable to God (see Romans 12:1).

Every believer has the responsibility to hear God for themselves. There are genuine men and women of God who can stand with us in prayer and share encouragement. However, the buck stops with us. By the way, every believer has the Holy Spirit. When Jesus promised to send us a Helper, He was making a divine investment in every child of God.

YOUR PURPOSE JOURNEY

As you mature, you realize your desperate need for the Helper (Holy Spirit). This will steer you away from over relying on the support of man which the Bible calls vain (Psalm 60:11). We also read about the futility of man's help in Jeremiah 17:5-8:

> Thus says the Lord: "Cursed is the man who trusts in man and makes flesh his strength, whose heart departs from the Lord. For he shall be like a shrub in the desert, and shall not see when good comes, but shall inhabit the parched places in the wilderness, in a salt land which is not inhabited.
>
> "Blessed is the man who trusts in the Lord, and whose hope is the Lord. For he shall be like a tree planted by the waters, which spreads out its roots by the river, and will not fear when heat comes; but its leaf will be green, and will not be anxious in the year of drought, nor will cease from yielding fruit" (NKJV).

Have you noticed there are perennial complainers who take issue with everyone and everything in life? If it is not the government, then it is their boss, or their spouse, or the children, or the church, or their housekeeper, or climate change ... the list is endless. If you live this way, when will you ever wake up, smell the roses, become part of the solution to life's challenges – and make hay while the sun shines? We must remain guided by John 9:4:

> "We must quickly carry out the tasks

assigned us by the one who sent us. The night is coming, and then no one can work" (NLT).

As a coach, I observe the growing need for balance between personal development and professional courses. In fact, I'm of the view that young people should first pursue personal development to understand themselves and their unique purpose before embarking on professional courses at degree, masters, or Ph.D level. One is better off getting professional certification in an area of your calling than simply getting a qualification for employment's sake.

For professionals in the job market, there is still an opportunity for personal development. As Marshall Goldsmith says, "What got you here won't get you there." For example, your academic prowess may have landed you a top position in a leading company. However, if you are abrasive and lack regard for others, you will not last. As Mr. Goldsmith says, "All other things being equal, your people skills (or lack of them) become more pronounced the higher up you go. In fact, even when all other things are not equal, your people skills often make the difference in how high you go." PDI offers various personal development packages for professionals such as emotional intelligence, self-awareness, leadership intelligence, etc.

It's said that all leaders are readers. Most people assume that this quote is for people who hold leadership positions. The truth is, everyone is a leader, and we can lead without a title or grand position. As John Maxwell says, "Leadership is influence!" Everyone has a measure of faith (Romans 12:3) and we all have a measure of influence too.

Do you now consider yourself a leader? Then you should be a reader! I have been a reader since childhood, and that is how I stayed out of trouble. After school, I'd do my house chores and then immerse myself in books. By the way, though there's a part of my personality style that is extroverted, the people who understand me intimately know that I am a deep-seated introvert. I'm good with a book while everyone else goes to a party!

One of the things that has helped me is reading Dr. Stanko's books along with those of other authors like my coach, Sally Mahihu, Lydia Jamenya, Myles Munroe and John Maxwell. I read across genres including spiritual, business, leadership, and financial books. At The Kingdom Connect we have a virtual book club. In the last three years, the community has tremendously developed themselves through a shared culture of reading. It's been a joy to note many virtual book clubs emerging in Kenya. We need to enourage a reading culture to shift leadership narratives.

Do not be deceived. There are no shortcuts to purpose or to Kingdom work.

Chapter Eight
PERSONALITY

John Stanko

Irene frequently refers to the DISC profile and the impact it had on her life when we met that March day at the Hilton Hotel. I can say the same thing, for God used the profile to help me understand who I am (and who I am not), which helped me identify my purpose and avoid distractions. I was so impacted by the profile in 1992 that I said to the Lord, "This was such a blessing. I would like to become certified and, if You will help me, use what I know to help other people." I did, He did, and I have.

That is the reason I introduced the profiles to Irene and many others in Kenya because I know how much we struggle as believers to talk about our strengths and weaknesses. The profiles help "prime the pump," so to speak, and get us in the flow of discussing our God-given personalities. Let me tell you more of my story so you will understand why and how the profile made such a difference.

In 1974 after graduate school, while working as a financial aid officer for a chain of trade schools, I began to prepare for the ministry. My pastor started to mentor me and expose me to the things I would need to be a successful pastor. I eventually enrolled in a seminary and received a masters and doctorate in pastoral ministries. In 1989, I became pastor of Covenant Church in Orlando, Florida, and pastored that church for four years.

There was only one problem. I found out that I didn't like pastoring. More than that, I discovered that pastoring didn't like me. I was a task-oriented individual functioning in a career and position that required a lot of people-oriented skills. While those skills could be (and were) learned, they still took a lot of energy and generated a lot of stress. I wasn't a happy leader because I wasn't leading where I could utilize my strengths to the fullest.

At the urging of a friend, I completed a profile called "The Personality System" published by The Institute for Motivational Living, Inc. in New Castle, Pennsylvania. This profile is also known by the acronym DISC because it identifies four behavioral styles that begin with the letters DISC. The D stands for dominant, driving, determined; the I for influencing, insightful, inspirational; the S for steady, stable, secure; and the C for compliant, correct, conscientious.

My original profile results showed that I was under tremendous stress and pressure trying to be all styles to all people. That's what the ministry can do to someone who feels the pressure to adapt to everyone's expectations, something I was trying to do to be a "good" pastor. The profile went on to show that I was a "C" style with a "D" style to back that up. I was a task-oriented individual who liked projects and tasks and the challenges that came with them.

The profile indicated that I was quite low in the "I" style and also low in the "S" style. In short, I functioned best in situations that required strong administrative and organizational skills, and less so in a situation that required a lot of interpersonal contact and nurture. I enjoyed working on a lot of different tasks at once and I thrived on change and constant challenges. In short, I wasn't cut out to be a pastor – at least not in the way I was trying to be one.

Armed with that information, I resigned the pastorate a few months later to take a job with Integrity Music as director of their conference and educational division. That began three of the happiest and most fulfilling years of my life. Whenever I have gone back in church work over the years, I'm more knowledgeable of who I am and who I'm not. I still did pastoral things, but I avoided being drawn into all the activities of the pastorate and maintained a good percentage of my time in the areas of administration, projects management, writing, traveling, and team building. Today I am not in a full-time ministry position, but I travel, consult, run a publishing company, and write. I love what I do and every day I feel challenged to learn, grow, and serve others in new, fresh ways. I am truly living my dream.

That DISC profile caused me to look at who

I was and wasn't. It's not a magic profile nor is it perfect or psychologically sophisticated. It was enough, however, to get me started on a path of self-understanding that has enhanced my leadership abilities. I stopped trying to be what I wasn't and began to strengthen and improve what I was. I have used it to help people follow the same path to purposeful living in their lives.

Also, you probably realize by now that Irene is predominantly a High-I style, and I am a High D and C style. That means we work well together as a team because we are so different. We complement one another, but we have to work to understand each other, for we will approach a similar project or idea from totally different perspectives. It requires us to communicate clearly and precisely, for it is easy for a High-I and a High-C to hear through the filter of their own style and that can cause problems. So far, we have been able to avoid any difficulties because we have good self-knowledge.

Peter Drucker's book, *Management Challenges for the 21st Century*, addresses the issue of self-knowledge. Drucker encourages leaders to develop feedback analysis. This is done by "whenever one makes a key decision, and whenever one does a key action, one writes down what they expect will happen. And nine or twelve months later one then feeds back from results or expectations."[5]

From this, Drucker summarizes three *action conclusions* from the feedback analysis:

1. **Concentrate on your strengths.** Place yourself where your strengths can produce your strengths.

2. **Work on improving your strengths.** The feedback analysis rapidly shows where a person needs to improve skills or has to acquire new knowledge. It will show where skills and knowledge are no longer adequate and have to be updated. It will also pinpoint gaps in your knowledge.
3. **Work to correct disabling ignorance.** This he describes as areas of weakness that undermine one's strengths.[6]

My profile not only helped me to identify my strengths but also to work on my own disabling ignorance. While my profile showed my task orientation, it also revealed how little I understood people who weren't like me, along with a paltry comprehension of where they were "coming from." That would have been true of my relationship with Irene. Before the profile, I would have avoided working with someone like her because that person wasn't organized enough for me. Those people were too "flighty," going from one project to the next, while I preferred to drill down deep, take my time, and finish what was started. I realized how rough I could be working with people who were motivated by relationships or routines – both of which represented my disabling ignorance.

After my profile session, I began to work on understanding (and I am still working at it) what motivated people unlike me and began to apply what I learned. I was still motivated by my strength of getting the job done, but I was complementing that strength by learning how to motivate people and win their support. In this way I made my strengths of project management more effective. I've had to improve my people skills if I was going to be fully productive because the projects I oversee all involve people. To not do that would be to render my strengths useless or less than they could be, and that wasn't acceptable to me.

In knowing myself, I've come to some other conclusions about who I am and am not. I've discovered that:

1. I love to travel, partly because of the challenge it presents that satisfies my "D" style and partly because it gives me uninterrupted chunks of time to read, write, and work on projects that require uninterrupted time.

2. I can work with people, but when I do, I need to schedule some "down time" somewhere after that to replenish and recharge my "batteries."

3. I am a morning person, working best in the early hours on writing and projects. I need to leave busy work, phone calls, meetings, and follow up for the afternoon.

4. I like working for a big organization where there are lots of activities and opportunities.

5. I'm a city person. I like traffic, people, and congestion. The mountains or nature hold no special blessing for me.

6. I prefer to watch as a way to learn, but I don't mind reading. For me, it's not either/or.

I've included those few personal likes and dislikes to show that I've worked on who I am, worked on knowing myself. I'm still learning, but I've taken seriously Drucker's challenge to self-knowledge:

> We will have to learn where we belong, what our strengths are, what we have to learn so that we get the full benefit from it, where our defects are, what we are not good at, where we belong, what our values are. For the first time in human history, we will have to learn to take responsibility for managing ourselves. This is probably a much bigger change than any technology – a change in the human condition. Nobody teaches it – no school or college – and it probably will be another hundred years before they teach it.[7]

In the meantime, the achievers – and I don't mean the millionaires, but rather the ones who want to make a contribution, who want to lead a fulfilling life, and want to feel that there is some purpose in their being on this earth – will have to learn something which, only a few years ago, only a few super achievers ever knew. They will have to learn to manage themselves, to build on their strengths, and to build on their values.

Do what you must do to learn about who you are and aren't. Build on your strengths and minimize your weaknesses. Don't rely on charisma or special talents to prop up your leadership position. Work to know yourself and then improve from that base of knowledge. That is what I have come to love and appreciate about Irene. She is totally committed to the self-knowledge process, and she works to better understand who she is and what makes her tick. That's why she has been so successful, and why I love working with her so much. She is my alter ego and I have learned as much from her as she claims she has from me. Thank you, Irene, for a life well-lived and for sharing it with me and so many others.

Chapter Nine

THE PROCESS OF CHANGE FOR PDI

Irene Mureithi

Dr. Stanko says I am his best student in the world. I am thankful for this recognition because I know he means it. I give God all the glory for helping me find my purpose.

The title of a "best student" only makes sense when I reflect of the many people who have clarified their purpose through the PDI programs in the last 13 years. I would say 85% of the people who came through the PDI classes have discovered their purpose and are flourishing in what they're doing. They too are touching many lives through their purpose. Watching the ripple effect has been an awesome and beautiful thing. It reminds me of God's instruction to all of us in Genesis 1:28:

> And God blessed them [granting them certain authority] and said to them, "Be fruitful, multiply, and fill the earth, and subjugate it [putting it under your power];

and rule over (dominate) the fish of the sea, the birds of the air, and every living thing that moves upon the earth."

Did you notice that the instruction was not to dominate one other? I imagine heaven must stop to admire when brethren live together in unity, serving each other through our various callings – while submitting one to another out of love, and not manipulation or control. Isn't this the Kingdom of God?

I remember PDI season three graduation at Amboseli Serena Hotel in 2011. We gathered for a bush dinner and as the stars and the moon joined in chorus, there were many discussions – and a surprise party for the late Dr. James Mageria who was celebrating his 70th birthday. He had joined us for the graduation with his beautiful wife, Mrs. Beatrice Mageria. A pilot who was also graduating together with his wife wrote a long testimonial saying the effect of the work we were doing at PDI would be felt 10 years later.

Looking back 10 years on, we thank God for every life that has been touched and is in turn touching many other lives. I am certain that God has great plans ahead but if this was it (and I pray I live to see the greater days ahead), my soul is satisfied that the legacy will live on in the hearts of men, women, and children.

There is a place in building generational wealth where people leave behind beautiful buildings. The vision God gave me for PDI was, and remains, to build people. In as much as we are building beautiful houses at Serian Country Homes, what will make this community truly outstanding are the transformed homeowners (many of whom have passed through PDI and TKC classes). In my view, there is nothing more handsome in a man or more beautiful in a woman than a life lived for God and in pursuit of a divine assignment. The peace and joy that being in your purpose gives are something divine. As you've already read in previous chapters, there have been many challenges (especially finances) yet still, I would not trade the purpose experience for gold or diamonds.

When I reflect on the inner harmony purpose gives, I can only think of this verse in Psalm 133:1-3:

> Behold, how good and how pleasant it is for brothers to dwell together in unity! It is like the precious oil [of consecration] poured on the head, coming down on the beard, even the beard of Aaron, coming down upon the edge of his [priestly] robes [consecrating the whole body]. It is like the dew of [Mount] Hermon coming down on the hills of Zion; for there the Lord has commanded the blessing: life forevermore.

The verse above describes the power of divine harmony among believers. This is the kind of unity we should have as the body of Christ, especially in the marketplace. I love watching presidential parades. Every soldier stands alert in their place of assignment. You don't see them crisscrossing the arena in an unorganized manner. They move in formation and great discipline. The Father is pleased to give us the Kingdom. Wouldn't it be amazing if He can watch us from

Heaven above as each one of us is positioned in our divine assignment just like the soldiers?

It's one thing to sing the Sunday School song, "I'm a soldier in the army of the Lord," and a whole other thing to trample aimlessly all over the marketplace with no sense of purpose, order, or discipline! And this is where Dr. Stanko's purpose comes in handy – creating order out of chaos. I wonder if the angels feel like joining Dr. Stanko to organize the army of God in the marketplace?

The truths shared in this book may be hard to hear, but the intention is not to harm you. Instead, it is to call us to order so we can execute God's end-time agenda for the world with discipline and finesse. In a season of gross darkness and global deception, we are the light of the world. We need to heed Prophet Isaiah's call to arise in Isaiah 60:1-2:

> "Arise [from spiritual depression to a new life], shine [be radiant with the glory *and* brilliance of the LORD]; for your light has come, and the glory *and* brilliance of the LORD has risen upon you. For in fact, darkness will cover the earth and deep darkness *will cover* the peoples; But the LORD will rise upon you [Jerusalem] and His glory *and* brilliance will be seen on you.

If there was ever a time in the history of the world where men and women of purpose are needed, it is now.

If you're familiar with the concept of the Seven Mountains of Influence originally introduced in 1975 by the late Bill Bright (founder of

Campus Crusade) and the late Loren Cunningham (founder of Youth With a Mission), you know that in every nation we need voices of truth in religion, family, education, government, media, arts and entertainment, and business. As earlier mentioned, we look forward to featuring PDI-TKC alumni on the TKC Show. Their stories will inspire and encourage you to be purpose driven.

The process of change at PDI is ongoing. Since 2010 when we opened our doors, we determined that the organization would build systems and structures to help us carry out our mandate. The work has involved many people because it was never designed as a one-man-show. We have received tons of written feedback that has helped us to improve our content and processes. At some point, we got the rhythm right on how to run physical classes, seminars, corporate trainings, church training, form four leavers' classes and more.

And then Covid-19 struck.

The structures we had established came in handy during the pandemic when we had to quickly transition to online classes. Our content remained largely the same, although we introduced totally new programs in response to our clients' need to build emotional, mental, spiritual, and financial resilience in this troubling period.

Coach Betty Mwaura, a PDI alumna, and I gave away 15 free live videos and introduced fairly-priced "Mindset and Money Makeover" classes. In addition, another way that PDI supported many people during the pandemic was by introducing a year-long online training where individuals would log in every Sunday night for only

US$50 for 12 months. The testimonials we have received from the participants of the TKC program are mind-boggling.

The second major change is in adapting to new media to tell our story and reach our audience. When we started PDI, we relied heavily on mainstream media (radio and TV) for our advertising and publicity. We slowly incorporated social media, specifically Facebook, and now we can say 80% of all our clients connect with us through various digital platforms. The new TKC Show is also promoted and flighted on social media, further signifying the importance of adapting to technological changes in business and in sharing the gospel.

I love social media and I'm grateful we have it. I appreciate how Dr. Stanko challenges people, especially church folk, to use social media more regularly and effectively. I definitely have a growing following now post-pandemic. I'm at 21,000 people following me and hoping to grow the numbers more.

Believers need to embrace social media and emerging technologies to amplify their life purpose message, as well as to spread the good news of the Kingdom of God. Have you noticed how the world courageously tells their story and shapes narratives using mainstream and social media? Never mind that most of their content is unpalatable and deceptive at best. They have no qualms rubbing it in your face either.

How much more should we who have received the words of eternal life from Jesus rise boldly, speak truth and wisdom fluently, and fill the airwaves with the message of the Kingdom of God? The more people we can reach in the world with what we have, the better they and the world will be. I'm committed to being authentic on social media, especially in the Kenyan space, because we have a lot of people using these platforms in what I consider fake and staged ways.

I love to proclaim that Jesus is Lord of the marketplace – and indeed He is! He has divine strategies that we can employ even in the world of business like He did with Simon Peter and his business at the water's edge in Luke 5:4-8.

> When He had finished speaking, He said to Simon [Peter], "Put out into the deep water and lower your nets for a catch [of fish]." Simon replied, "Master, we worked hard all night [to the point of exhaustion] and caught nothing [in our nets], but at Your word I will [do as you say and] lower the nets [again]." When they had done this, they caught a great number of fish, and their nets were [at the point of] breaking; so they signaled to their partners in the other boat to come and help them. And they came and filled both of the boats [with fish], so that they began to sink. But when Simon Peter saw this, he fell down at Jesus' knees, saying, "Go away from me, for I am a sinful man, O Lord!"

The pandemic also debunked the idea that everyone had to work from the office to be productive. While in many developed nations work from home was a concept that was embraced decades ago, in Kenya (and largely other parts of Africa) it's the pandemic that ushered in this new way of working. It was a pleasant surprise when corporate Kenya engaged PDI to train their staff online. This has continued to this day and as the world has transitioned out of the pandemic, we are now working with a hybrid model. Some organizations have requested in-person staff training, while others still prefer to engage online.

Globally, many organizations had to learn how to work online. I am still surprised at how connected people feel during the online PDI classes. The chat sessions in Zoom, Google Meet, and Microsoft Teams come alive as people engage. Sometimes it's even more lively than it would be in a physical session because ordinarily only one person at a time can ask questions or give feedback during a physical class.

However, in online classes, so many people engage in the chat at the same time, making the classes very lively. There is great learning not only from the facilitator, but also among the students themselves. In addition, introverted attendees can contribute as they find it a safe space using the keyboard. The outspoken ones naturally prefer to voice their thoughts and contributions. Their virtual hands are the first to go up. The upside? Everyone learns and contributes. I found that it works very well and I'm enjoying this season. I guess that means there is a positive side of Covid.

I thank Dr. Stanko for introducing me to the DISC profile. It changed my life. Now PDI also offers DISC online and this has enabled us to have clients in the diaspora. Many times I ordered physical DISC booklets through Dr. Stanko. I no longer do this because all the childrens, teens, and adult assessments are available online.

Change is the only constant, and even then, it is not easy. Even for me as a coach, initially there was resistance to change because of being accustomed to doing things a certain way. Who knows what the online space is going to be in the next ten years? There's so much talk of transitions and all that is happening with Artificial Intelligence (AI). But whatever comes now because of, and after Covid, let's get ready to ride the waves.

In the previous paragraphs, I have talked about changes from the outside world that have enabled us to adapt internally. I believe that another wave of change is coming that will empower PDI-TKC to influence from the inside-out.

When running DISC, children and teens always ask why it is not part of the school curriculum. This is a call to us as PDI-TKC to influence the mountain of education. We've had the privilege to coach children from public and private schools representing different curricula like:

- The International General Certificate of Secondary Education (IGCSE)
- Accelerated Christian Education (ACE)
- International Baccalaureate (IB) and the
- Competency Based Curriculum, which covers the Kenya Certificates of Primary and Secondary Education (KCPE/KCSE).

We look forward to greater days ahead as we become part of the solution that the government is looking for in matters of competency-based education in Kenya. We have a dream that DISC will be part of the school curriculum in Kenya because young people truly love and enjoy it. It sets them free to be who God created them to be.

DISC is a powerful tool even in the corporate world. We at PDI recently had the privilege to conduct online one-to-one sessions for a leading organization and later an in-person engagement for the entire group. We have always received great feedback on how the TEAMS, VALUES, and DISC profiles help in team building. The fact that each staff member receives their three-in-one report and can share their results among themselves willingly improves team culture and communication.

Some people are assertive, results-oriented, and seek out challenges. Others are outgoing, persuasive, optimistic, and people-oriented. There are those who seek stability, prefer working at a steady, even pace, and are reserved. Then there are team members who prefer to work with facts, accuracy, systems, and structures at both work and life. This kind of self-awareness and adaptability helps people enjoy their time at work in corporate set ups. The same is true for people running their own businesses, as well as for ministry teams in churches. Our foundation at Personal Development Institute is based on Romans 12:2:

> And do not be conformed to this world [any longer with its superficial values and customs], but be transformed and

progressively changed [as you mature spiritually] by the renewing of your mind [focusing on godly values and ethical attitudes], so that you may prove [for yourselves] what the will of God is, that which is good and acceptable and perfect [in His plan and purpose for you].

Our other anchoring verse is found in Proverbs 23:7:

> "For as he thinketh in his heart, so is he" (KJV).

From both Scriptures, we see that transformation is a result of thinking new thoughts. I believe there can be no real change without new thinking. There's a course we've run since 2011 called "Think, Shift, and Change" that addresses the issue of mindset change from a Kingdom perspective.

A good example is the story of Jabez who was born in pain and cried out to God for enlargement of his territory. He refused to be defined by his pain because he embraced new ways of thinking, as we see in 1 Chronicles 4:9-10:

> Jabez was more honorable than his brothers; but his mother named him Jabez, saying, "Because I gave birth to him in pain." Jabez cried out to the God of Israel, saying, "Oh that You would indeed bless me and enlarge my border [property], and that Your hand would be with me, and You would keep me from evil so that it does not hurt me!" And God granted his request.

The Kingdom Connect (TKC), which is one of the new programs at Personal Development Institute, is anchored on Colossians 1:27:

> God [in His eternal plan] chose to make known to them how great for the Gentiles are the riches of the glory of this mystery, which is Christ in and among you, the hope and guarantee of [realizing the] glory.

We recognize that when all is said and done on this side of eternity, be it in our homes, businesses, marketplace, society, and the nations at large, Christ in us is the hope of glory. And so shall Revelation 11:15 come to pass:

> Then the seventh angel sounded: And there were loud voices in heaven, saying, "The kingdoms of this world have become the kingdoms of our Lord and of His Christ, and He shall reign forever and ever!" (NKJV).

As I sign off, allow me to invite you to the glorious Kingdom of our God through Jesus Christ. I also extend an invitation for you to consider joining us in the PDI-TKC classes.

Chapter Ten
CREATIVITY

John Stanko

I don't think Irene has mentioned creativity specifically in her story, but it is implied throughout. Her teaching ability is certainly part of her creativity as is her tremendous sense of fashion along with her flair for business. When she founded PDI and now all the various classes and trainings, they were expressions of her creativity. Her response to the pandemic that has taken her much more deeply into online training is another result of her ability to create something out of nothing. Her fertile mind coupled with her High-I personality style are always producing thoughts of doing new things in fresh, innovative ways.

I am writing a chapter on creativity because of its importance in finding and fulfilling your life purpose. When I first described my purpose, it was "to *bring* order out of chaos." I want you to keep the word *bring* in mind as I proceed. Over the course of my adult career, I didn't see myself as a creative person and would say so to anyone who cared to listen. I thought of myself as an administrator who could fix problems but not as a creator who could start new things. My thinking of creativity, at that time, was thinking or doing something the world had never seen before, sort of like Einstein who came up with a formula that no one else had produced.

Then one day in 2006 or so, I was in Zimbabwe, driving to the office at the church where I was consulting, and had, for lack of a better term, a significant spiritual experience. I was thinking about the concept of creativity when the Lord spoke to me: "You don't *bring* order out of chaos, you *create* order out of chaos. *You* are a creative person!" It was as if the Lord was in the car with me and I heard an audible voice so clearly that I turned around to make sure there was no one in the backseat. *I was a creative person. I am creative!* Those thoughts flooded my mind, and I can still see my hands trembling on the steering wheel.

My experience did not end when I arrived at the office, for I kept thinking about what I had heard and continued to tremble throughout the day. Then as I settled down, I reflected on my life and began to see that the declaration was indeed true: I had been and was a creative person. I had started playing violin when I was eight years old and became quite proficient. I did not have a lot of friends to play with, so I found ways to play by myself. I created a baseball league and would throw a ball against the stone wall at our home, actually pretending that two teams were playing one another. I would field the ball as it came off the wall, or at times it would fly over my head, but each throw and resulting bounce back counted as outs or runs. I kept score, maintained the standings of wins and losses, and had playoffs at the end of the summer before school began. I was creative!

Then as an adult, I was an event planner, a writer (of letters and assigned articles, seldom anything on my own initiative), and a humorist (I had been able to make people laugh from the time I was four years old). I saw that all those were creative expressions. When I heard the voice in 2006, I had started two companies, had written six books, consulted, coached, counseled, developed workshops and seminars, and had championed the purpose message along with a message on servant leadership through my writing and speaking – something few believers were doing as I was also an early adopter of social media.

This revelation changed my life and the way I saw myself, and I was so excited that I knew I had to share what I had learned with my following through the *Monday Memo*, my blog, and my online Bible studies (which, by the way, were other creative expressions). Who was among the first I heard from when I started writing on creativity? It was none other than Irene, who urged me to teach on creativity, and when I came to Kenya, we did some media interviews that focused on the topic.

As I look back, I shouldn't have been surprised that I had my epiphany where creativity is concerned. It seems like once people overcome their hesitancy and fear to find and express their purpose, creativity is not far behind. It's like purpose is locked up in a cage, and when they opened the door, creativity jumped out before the cage door was closed. I was coaching one woman to help her find purpose and we made great progress. Then one day, she said, "I have some poems. They're not very good but I've written them over the years and never shown them to anyone. Could I show them to you?"

When I asked her how many poems she had, she replied, "Hundreds." When I read them, they were quite good and she has taken steps to use them more in her ministry, but she isn't ready to publish them yet. My point is that creativity is often connected to purpose, for people of purpose will find new, fresh ways to do what it is they were created to do (created to be creators by the Creator). That is what I have done, for I have invented many new approaches and programs to help others create order out of their chaos and find purpose. And now I have a publishing company that not only publishes what I write but also what others have written. And God has opened a door for my books to now be printed and distributed in Kenya – an answer to a long-time prayer request.

The concept of creativity is found in the earliest part of the Old Testament, Genesis 2 to be exact. It is there that God directed Adam's work but allowed Adam to express his creativity:

> Now the Lord God had formed out of the ground all the wild animals and all the birds in the sky. He brought them to the man to see what he would name them; and whatever the man called each living

creature, that was its name. So the man gave names to all the livestock, the birds in the sky and all the wild animals. But for Adam no suitable helper was found (Genesis 2:19-20).

I've discovered that we as believers are a bit ambivalent about our role and God's role in creativity. We're fearful of doing something outside of God's will, so we often describe our creativity as purely a function of God's leadership. Therefore, I hear people say when talking about their creative expressions, "The Lord spoke to me; the Lord directed me; the Lord laid on my heart; God inspired me. God gave me these poems or songs," always careful not to indicate any personal initiative in what they did.

I believe God does "speak, direct, lay on hearts, and inspire" but I don't believe He does that for *every* creative expression. Otherwise, we're simply robots or secretaries taking down God's dictation. If you have a six-line poem, does God have to be the One who initiated that? Is it possible for you to decide to express your creativity and then do it? Part of the problem is our fear of failure, of mis-representing God, of seeming like we have an ego or free will.

I often point out that we cannot help but inject ourselves into the creative process, for often when people give me things the Lord "gave them," there are misspelled words and bad grammar. So if God "gave" that to them, in jest I ask if that means He isn't a very good writer or speller? Of course not! It means that even when His creative ideas flow through us, they are subject to our limitations. However, we work to reduce or eliminate those limitations (like becoming better spellers), and our work improves.

In Genesis 2, God didn't bring an animal to Adam, only to have Adam stare at it dumbfounded, at which point God whispered in his ear, "Cow," to which Adam said, "Cow. We will name this a cow," and God responded, "Good job, Adam!" That isn't what happened, and if it did, it would not have been Adam's creativity. There's no question that man's fall marred and polluted our creativity, but Jesus came to reconcile all things to the Father, and that includes our creativity. We can be creative and *not* be outside of God's will, *unless* we commandeer our creativity to use solely as we see fit, not making it available to God's direction and use.

Since I accepted the adjustment in my purpose statement from I *"bring"* order to *"create"* order, my creativity has exploded. I now have more than 80 books to my credit, including two fiction, twelve volumes of a verse-by-verse New Testament commentary and five volumes of an Old Testament devotional commentary. I maintain five Facebook pages, write every day, post a daily devotional seven days a week, and started Urban Press, the publishing company I mentioned earlier, which is the publisher for this book.

I started the publishing company to help people express their creativity as it jumped out of the cage as I described earlier. I sit with people and develop and edit their manuscripts, and I hold their hand as they navigate the minefield of creative expression. I've seen people produce a completed book manuscript, only to have them get cold feet just as we were about to publish, and the main culprit was fear – the same enemy trying to prevent them from finding purpose. I've learned how to face and manage my fear, and I help other people do the same.

Since 2001, I have written what I call *The Monday Memo*. I developed the *Memo* in response to many people who would hear my purpose message and say, "We need more help. We wish we had you around more to talk to so we could bounce things off you to see if we are on the right track." Also, I was about to launch a website and thought, *What reason would anyone have to come to my website except to check it out when it is launched?* I thought if I wrote a *Memo* every week, people would be reminded of the purpose message and could then access the many resources on my site. As of this writing, I have written more than 1,100 *Monday Memos* and converted their content into 15 books.

At first, I was afraid (yes, there is fear again) that I would run out of material or that I would get bored or, worse yet, the readers would get tired of it. To my surprise, none of that has happened. It has been a great exercise in faith to sit down every Sunday night for more than 20 years and trust God to help me produce something that would assist people anywhere in the world who wanted to find and fulfill their purpose.

In my next chapter, I will share a few *Monday Memos* with you that are pertinent to this book, but also to give you an idea of what they look like to stimulate your creativity. Let me add

YOUR PURPOSE JOURNEY

that Kenya still has more Monday Memo readers than any other country, even the United States. That's another indication of how the purpose message impacted the Kenyan people. You will see that each *Memo* is only seven or eight paragraphs, so they are pretty short and to the point.

Let's look at a few of them now and I want you to pray as you read them, "Lord, how can I take what I know and who I am and share them with the world?" As you pray, I know God will help you take the next step to express your creativity as you confront your fears of doing so.

Chapter Eleven
THE MONDAY MEMO

John Stanko

In my last chapter, I promised to share with you some of my *Monday Memos* from the archive that I have been producing every week since March of 2001. They have included insight into purpose, along with *Memos* on creativity, leadership, goal-setting, and faith. Here is the first *Memo* I ever wrote.

The Monday Memo
from the desk of
Dr. John W. Stanko
Issue One

Hello and welcome to this first edition of the *Monday Memo*. My objective in writing is to help you focus this week on an issue that makes you more productive and fulfilled in your walk with the Lord. I am writing to you this week from Birmingham, England where I have been speaking on purpose and then conducting one-on-one interviews with people who are seeking to know who they are. I have been reminded this past week of what Laurence Boldt wrote, which is also mentioned in my book, *I Wrote This Book on Purpose,*

> We make some attempt to answer them [the questions "who am I?" and "why am I here?"]. We ask our parents and teachers and it seems they do not know. They refer us to political and religious institutions, which often crank out canned answers devoid of personal meaning. Some even tell us that life has no meaning, save for eating and breeding. Most of us are smart enough to recognize that canned answers or begging the question will not do. We must find real answers for ourselves. But that takes more heart and effort than we are often willing to give.

How much are you willing to "give" this week to define who you are and who you are not. Can you spend 15 minutes a day? Can you ask those closest to you how they see you and what they think your strengths are? If you are willing to spend the time, prayerfully and diligently pursue the answers to these questions:

1. What situations seem to seek you out that you don't have to go looking for? Is there a problem that always finds its way to you to be solved? A certain type of person to which you find yourself drawn and effective? What kinds of jobs or ministries have given you the most joy?

2. What have people given you compliments about over the years that you don't think are very spiritual or special? Very often those hold clues to your purpose.
3. Is there a passage of Scripture that is especially meaningful to you because it summarizes who you are and what you do best?

May I suggest a purpose journal where you can record the answers to these questions over time. I leave you with some verses from the book of Proverbs:

> My son [or daughter], if you accept my words and store up my commands within you, turning your ear to wisdom and applying your heart to understanding, and if you call out for insight and cry aloud for understanding, and if you look for it as for silver and search for it as for hidden treasure, then you will understand the fear of the Lord and find the knowledge of God (Proverbs 2:2-4).

Seek and keep on seeking your purpose. Don't give up and the Lord will reward you with clarity and direction.

Yours on purpose,
John Stanko
Gold Mine Development Company

******

Notice that I signed off from a company

YOUR PURPOSE JOURNEY

called Gold Mine Development Company, because I named my company after my first book, *Life is a Gold Mine*, before I changed it to PurposeQuest, Inc. Now let's look at *Memo #14*:

> The Monday Memo
> from the desk of Dr. John Stanko
> June 18, 2001 – Issue Fourteen

I receive a lot of questions every week, and most of them focus on the issue of life purpose. Over the years, the questions asked most often, along with my answers, are as follows:

Q. Can my purpose change over time?
A. No. How you fulfill your purpose may change, but your purpose remains the same. I have fulfilled my purpose, which is to bring order out of chaos, in a number of different job roles. My purpose is the same; how I do it may change.

Q. Can I have more than one purpose?
A. No. You can have many gifts and talents, or different ways to express or fulfill your purpose, but your purpose is a clear, simple summary of your essence that is singular.

Q. Should or can a husband and wife have the same purpose?
A. No. While it's possible for a couple to have the same purpose, I've found it to be rare. Even if both work in the same business, mission, or ministry, each partner will have a different purpose, a different function in the same organization.

Usually those purposes complement one another.

Q. What is the difference between a gift and purpose?
A. A gift is like a tool that you carry with you to help fulfill your purpose. A plumber's purpose is not to "wrench." The wrench helps the plumber achieve their purpose to repair or build. Your gifts do the same for you, but they're not to be confused with your purpose.

Q. What is the difference between my ministry and my purpose?
A. I want to focus on this answer for the remainder of this *Monday Memo*. Too often we are tempted to separate what we do in church from what we do outside of it. We tend to think of ministry as related to church work, and purpose as something that may or may not fit into our church role. I contend that there's no difference between the two.

    I met with a man in Atlanta, Georgia once who has had a career in the field of human resources. Yet he was clearly a pastor. When I suggested that perhaps he was a chaplain or pastor in his company, he rejected the idea at first because he didn't have a pulpit or like public speaking. Yet he clearly had cared and "shepherded" people for his entire corporate career. By the end of our meeting, he began to see his purpose was to care for people in a business setting. He then realized his purpose *was* his ministry; it just wasn't taking place within the walls of a church building. That knowledge set him free to be who God made him to be because he no longer saw his ministry and purpose as two different things.

Perhaps you aren't clear about your purpose because you've put God in a box. You're a prophet, but everyone knows that prophets only function in a church setting. Who said that? Who said you can't bring the word of the Lord as a prophet to situations outside the church? Or perhaps you bring healing and wholeness to people, but don't lay hands on anyone or do it within a church. Does that limit your purpose or usefulness to God? Maybe you a teacher or preacher, but your pulpit is in a school or hospital? I met a man once whose title was school principal or headmaster, but he came to see his purpose was to pastor the children who attended his school along with their parents.

As we close, read the words of Robert Greenleaf and be free to minister (which simply means to serve) in whatever setting the Lord chooses for you, whether it's in or outside the church:

> The great religious prophets of the future will not necessarily be theologians, philosophers, or people of literature. They are as likely to be lawyers, doctors, businesspeople, scientists, or politicians. And they will carry out their prophetic roles while functioning at a high level of excellence in their professional field. In fact, unless significant prophecy emerges in all of these places, the vision, without which the people perish, will not be sufficiently evident.
>
> The world society in which we are all

inextricably involved is far too complex, it is in too revolutionary a mood, and it is fast becoming too literate and aware of its sources of expertise for very much of the prophetic wisdom it needs to be uttered by ministers, scholars, or writers. These will, of course, continue to serve, but more on a par with those who are more immersed in the ongoing work of the world.

Businesses, government bureaus, law firms, clinics, and scientific laboratories have not only become large, sophisticated institutions and important sources of new knowledge, but they are just as likely to harbor a philosopher, a prophet, or a saint as is the monastery or the university. *Seeker and Servant: Reflections on Religious Leadership.*

I hope this week you will find new peace to be who God made you to be in the setting that is best suited for you.

*****

Now here are two of my more popular *Monday Memos* that people have referred to again and again:

Early Edition of *The Monday Memo*
from the desk of Dr. John Stanko
Issue 19

I met with a man named Michael this week who has read my books. The church he attends was in part founded on the purpose message that he and others had read about, and now he is employed there. But when I asked him what his purpose was, he said, "I'm not sure." So I did what I always do: I started asking questions.

It didn't take long for me to hear some key words: *music, excellence,* and *projects* were a few. But then one phrase jumped out at me. He said, "I like to make things sing." What a colorful phrase. He wasn't saying that everything had to be musical. "Making everything sing" stated his commitment to excellence in whatever he did. He didn't want things to "hum" or "whistle;" he wanted every project, whether musical or not, to be the best expression of their unique purpose. I left Michael to consider whether or not his life purpose is to make things sing.

I received many purpose inquiries this past week from people needing help finding their purpose. It occurred to me that I found my purpose—to bring order out of chaos—when I read those words in a book. Those words "jumped out" at me and I was never the same. I thought this week I would provide some phrases for you to study to see if the same thing would happen to you.

I found the list below in a book entitled, *Whistle While You Work: Heeding Your Life's Calling* by Richard Leider and David A. Shapiro. The authors refer to this as a list of "Calling Cards," a concept they developed to help people like you and me find our life's calling and purpose. They explain:

> Each of these callings describes a core gift. Each calling comes directly from

someone's experience. We have been collecting callings in seminars, workshops, and coaching sessions with individuals and groups from all walks of life. The list of 52 callings we have come up with represent the "essence of essences" in our research. (This doesn't mean that there are not callings other than our 52; it does, however, mean that these 52 represent those that have best withstood real-world testing.) – page 35.

I'm including half of their list this week and I will send the other half next week. Study both lists and see if anything stirs you. Feel free to focus on one of these phrases that seems a close description of who you are. Allow God to "energize" that statement and make it your own. Or modify it in some way to make it a better fit for you. I hope the Lord will do for you what He did for me: By taking someone else's words, I was able to define my purpose. Happy seeking.

List of Calling Cards

Category: Realistic

1) building things; 2) fixing things; 3) growing things; 4) making things work; 5) shaping environments; 6) solving problems

Category: Conventional

1) doing the numbers; 2) getting things right; 3) operating things; 4) organizing things; 5) processing things; 6) straightening things up

YOUR PURPOSE JOURNEY

Category: Investigative

1) advancing ideas; 2) analyzing information; 3) investigating things; 4) getting to the heart of matters; 5) putting the pieces together; 6) researching things; 7) translating things; 8) discovering resources; 9) making connections

*****
The Monday Memo
from the desk of
Dr. John Stanko
Issue 20

I suppose if I had lived in Alaska, my first book would have been titled, *Life is a Gold Mine: Can You Pan It?* as opposed to *Can You Dig It?* The early Alaskan settlers panned for gold in Alaska's streams and rivers in hopes of finding their golden treasure. With that in mind, I decided to try my hand at gold panning one time while on my Alaskan cruise in a town called Skagway. More on where I panned later.

I did indeed find about ten small pieces of gold during my panning experience. And I found that if you're digging or panning for gold, it's certainly similar to what we go through to find our life purpose. How so? Consider these similarities:

1. You can pan on your own, but having someone with you who knows how to do it is a great help. My guide Tom began panning two years ago. He taught

us the proper procedures that enabled each one of us to find gold. When you are looking for your purpose, it often helps to involve other people. Ask them what they think your purpose may be. Better yet, find someone who knows their purpose and ask them to help you find yours.
2. **Panning is hard work.** I stood over a trough for a few minutes panning for the gold I found and my back ached. I thought about those who panned in the cold Alaskan weather, standing in cold water, and bending over for most of the day—hoping to strike it rich. Finding your purpose can be hard work, too; there's no guarantee when you'll find it or what you'll go through to discover the big golden nugget called purpose.
3. **You don't need a lot of tools.** You only need a pan to pan for gold, not a lot of sophisticated equipment. That's how it is as you search for your purpose. You start where you are, with what you have, and look in faith.
4. **You can't see the gold right away.** When I began panning, my pan was filled with dirt and gravel. That's how it is when you search for your purpose; you can't see the "gold" because of all the other "stuff" in your life. It's there, however, and you simply have to be

patient, keep seeking, know how to find it – and what you're looking for.
5. **It's exciting when you find the gold.** When I found the gold at the bottom of my pan, I felt like I was rich! When you find your life purpose, you feel the same way. The God of the universe knows who you are and gave you something to do that's just right for you.
6. **The gold stays in the pan.** Gold is so heavy that it's almost impossible to lose it when you're panning, while the lighter dirt and pebbles are easily eliminated. Your life purpose is the same way; it's a part of you that goes with you wherever you are, and is relevant no matter what mistakes you've made.

Last week I promised to give you the second half of the "Calling Cards" from the book entitled, *Whistle While You Work: Heeding Your Life's Calling* by Richard Leider and David A. Shapiro. If you just joined *The Monday Memo* family this week, the authors refer to the list below as "Calling Cards," a concept they developed to help people like you and me find our life's calling and purpose. They explain:

> Each of these callings describes a core gift. Each calling comes directly from someone's experience. We have been collecting callings in seminars, workshops, and coaching sessions with individuals and groups from all walks of life. The list of 52 callings we have come up with represent

the "essence of essences" in our research. (This doesn't mean that there are not callings other than our 52; it does, however mean that these 52 represent those that have best withstood real-world testing.) – page 35.

So are you ready to pan for gold? Put these calling cards in your pan and swirl them around to see if any stay in the bottom as the gold of your life. If you're not sure, then keep swirling them around in your mind and heart. Keep looking and I promise you'll find the riches that lie in all the "stuff" in your life. I hope it all pans out!

Category: Enterprising

1) bringing out potential; 2) empowering others; 3) exploring the way; 4) making deals; 5) managing things; 6) opening doors; 7) persuading people; 8) selling intangibles; 9) starting things

Category: Social

1) awakening spirit; 2) bringing joy; 3) building relationships; 4) creating dialogue; 5) creating trust; 6) facilitating change; 7) getting participation; 8) giving care; 9) healing wounds; 10) helping overcome obstacles; 11) instructing people; 12) resolving disputes

Category: Artistic

1) adding humor; 2) breaking molds; 3) creating things; 4) composing things; 5) designing things;

YOUR PURPOSE JOURNEY

6) moving through space; 7) performing events; 8) seeing possibilities; 9) seeing the big picture; 10) writing things

*****

I have to confess that I thoroughly enjoyed going back through the first 20 *Memos* I wrote, and I included more of them in this chapter than I anticipated because they're still good teaching tools. I can see why the *Memo* has lasted for as long as it has. It is regular (people can count on it showing up) and it has had useful content.

Chapter Twelve
THE FUNNEL PROCESS

John Stanko

After I taught on the concept of purpose for a few years, I had someone advise me that I needed to broaden my repertoire of messages. He felt I was getting too narrow in my thinking if I was going to be a successful teacher or consultant, I needed more. I considered this man's advice and felt like I did have more already. I had written and taught about what I called the five Gold Mine Principles of purpose, creativity, goals, time management, and faith. I also taught about such topics as leadership in general (servant leadership in particular), our mind as the source of personal transformation, and all sorts of Bible study topics (leadership, Proverbs, and the Psalms, just to name a few).

While I was grateful for this man's advice, I rejected it and instead decided to dig down even deeper into the concept of purpose. I determined that I was going to be one of the best purpose coaches and authors in the world by devoting myself to study, counseling, coaching, and writing. I found that this focus didn't limit me, but rather opened up the entire world of those who could benefit from my purpose of creating order out of chaos.

I've found that some people are hesitant to pursue identifying their purpose because, like my friend, they believe it is too restrictive, that it will limit what they can do, thus making them useful in only certain situations. However, I've found the opposite to be true and I wrote about it in a *Monday Memo*, which I include a portion of here:

The Funnel Process

A funnel is wide at the top and very narrow at the bottom so that liquids may be poured into something with a small opening. When you begin your PurposeQuest, you are at the top of the funnel. The whole world and all its options are available to you. Then something happens and it can unnerve you and make you uncomfortable. As you progress down the funnel of purpose, you may begin to feel restricted in your activity. Things you once did have no meaning or you lose your enthusiasm for things you once had energy to do. You also may find that you evaluate everything you do differently. As you go down the funnel, you find there's no room or time to do some of those things that are no longer related to your purpose.

Some are concerned that their lives will be less meaningful if they get to the bottom of the funnel. They can't see how God can use them when they seem to be doing so little. To the contrary, the bottom of the funnel is your point of greatest effectiveness. It's at that point where you find what you do that no one else can do. While it seems restrictive, that point allows God to send you anywhere in the world that needs who you are and what you do. The narrow point is why the funnel exists; without it, there would be no purpose for the larger, top portion of the funnel.

God is narrowing my activity so I can be more effective with greater impact. My pruning that is restricting my activities is actually making me more focused. As of this book, I have written and published 80 books of my own and helped more than 100 authors publish theirs by serving as their creative consultant and editor. I launched a mobile app that includes many hours of teaching, mostly video, and I find that I am also speaking more on leadership issues, which leads to opportunities to consult with and coach those who want to be better leaders. I was able to do all that because I stopped doing other things – like teaching at a university, being a radio talk show host, and part-time employee for a few businesses.

What are you holding on to that is restricting the funnel process in your own life? Is your fear that you won't have any money, causing you to hold on to some activities that have lost their life and interest for you? I urge you to follow my lead and embark on a self-pruning journey. Allow God to take you to new places that will lead to new fruitfulness as you let go of things that are important and dear but cannot make the trip down your funnel with you as seek your point of maximum potential and usefulness.

I mention an important word you should remember in the excerpt above, and that word is *pruning*. When God prunes us, we often feel like we have done something wrong and have missed Him in some way. To the contrary, God prunes us when we are fruitful and His goal is to make us even more fruitful, as Jesus explained:

> "I am the true vine, and my Father is the gardener. He cuts off every branch in me that bears no fruit, while every branch that does bear fruit he prunes so that it will be even more fruitful. You are already clean because of the word I have spoken to you. Remain in me, as I also remain in you. No branch can bear fruit by itself; it must remain in the vine. Neither can you bear fruit unless you remain in me.
>
> "I am the vine; you are the branches. If you remain in me and I in you, you will bear much fruit; apart from me you can do nothing. If you do not remain in me, you are like a branch that is thrown away and withers; such branches are picked up, thrown into the fire and burned. If you remain in me and my words remain in you, ask whatever you wish, and it will be done for you. This is to my Father's glory, that you bear much fruit, showing yourselves to be my disciples" (John 15:1-8).

Our relationship with the Lord isn't just about going to church or behaving ourselves – although both are important practices. Our relationship with Him is to bear fruit, and that's why purpose and creativity are so important – along with an understanding of our personality and how we will approach our work and other people.

This leads me to two questions I want to ask you: What is your fruit? Can you describe it? Jesus warned in Matthew 21:43: "Therefore I tell you that the kingdom of God will be taken away from you and given to a people who will produce its fruit." Let me go to another *Monday Memo* to discuss this concept of fruit.

The Fruit Process

I reflected recently on what it takes for actual, edible fruit to be produced. Here are some thoughts on the matter:

1. Fruit is fragile and conditions must be right for it to come forth—climate, soil, free from frost, not too much rain (or too little). The same is true for spiritual fruit.
2. Fruit starts with a blossom, which is pretty and fragrant, but is only the beginning. There are many believers who blossom and have great potential to bear fruit, but that potential must be nurtured.
3. If fruit is eaten before it's ripe, it can be toxic if harvested prematurely. The same is true for spiritual fruit. It requires maturity for it to taste the best.
4. Fruit is meant for two things: to be consumed by others or to produce seed so that more fruit can be produced. All spiritual fruit is for the benefit of other people to consume as they need it.
5. Fruit usually has a short lifespan and

must be consumed quickly so it won't go to waste. No one knows how many days they have to bear fruit, so it must be produced and distributed with a sense of urgency.
6. Fruit requires an ongoing process of pruning and fertilizing its source, or bad or anemic fruit will be produced. Believers must continue to nurture themselves spiritually if they're to continue to bear more and better fruit.

The Research Is In And ...

I spent some time reading what others have written about fruit and one thing is for certain: Most people have described what fruit is like (just as I did above) but they are hesitant to come out and say what we should be looking for in our lives that can be called fruit. Some say that it's souls saved or people we lead to the Lord, yet if truth be told, most people don't lead many others to the Lord. Others say it's a vibrant prayer life, but is fruit defined as the number of prayers a believer says in their lifetime? I don't think so. Finally, some identify fruit as correct doctrine, but that makes fruit an intellectual pursuit.

Lest all I do is judge what others have done and not contribute to the discussion, below I offer my definition of Kingdom fruit, and challenge you to identify what this fruit is in your life. Once you identify it, then I challenge you to determine how you can be even more fruitful. But first, here's my definition:

following your joy as you combine your

God-given gifts, creativity, purpose, experience, interests, and sustained effort in a way that produces something of value for the benefit of others and yourself.

My fruit is comprised of the books I've written; the libraries and school I've helped establish in Kenya; the classes I've taught at university; the devotionals I've written, published, and posted on social media for 16 years; and the seminars I've conducted on purpose and creativity. Oh yes, and as the Spirit has produced His fruit in my life, it has translated into tangible expressions of empathy for others in painful and difficult situations to which I formerly paid little attention.

Let me close with this thought: All fruit is measurable and measured. We speak of fruit as a cluster, a bunch, peck, half-bushel, bushel, pound, kilo, acre, or hectare. Therefore, I conclude that our fruit, even though it's spiritual, must be measurable as well. Spend some time praying and thinking about the question, "What is my fruit?" and then follow the answer up with another: "How can I produce more of it?" If you persevere in seeking the answers, you'll bear the fruit of the Kingdom in your life that God expects and enjoys. Don't be afraid of the funnel effect either, for it's God's way of narrowing your focus so you can maximize your effectiveness in the time you have left on earth.

Chapter Thirteen
THE FEAR FACTOR
John Stanko

As I close out my contributions to this book, I want to talk about the number one public enemy to your purpose and creativity and that quite simply is fear. Fear has us all in its grip and the problem is we don't know it – or don't want to face it. We don't know because fear doesn't show up in a monster mask making growling noises. It's quite rational and seems perfectly reasonable when we express it. "I don't have time" is a straightforward statement that everyone can relate to, and no one can challenge. Yet that simple phrase is a fear statement if you're considering doing something.

Let me explain. In reality, you have all the time in the world – 24 hours every day. You have the same amount of time as the richest or poorest person in the world. When you say, "I don't have time to write my book or go to school," you're really saying, "I'm *afraid* I don't have time to do those things the way I want them done. I'm afraid I will fail, or people will laugh at me because I didn't have the time to make my creative work perfect," but rather than say or face those things, we shorten it to "I don't have time."

When you use the excuse, "I don't want to get ahead of the Lord," or "I'm praying about it," those also sound reasonable and spiritual. Yet those statements are also fear-based. "I am afraid to get ahead of the Lord" and "I'm praying because I'm afraid what's in my heart is bad or not in God's will, and He'll be angry if I step out and do it." I advise people who tell me they can't find their purpose or achieve their creative goal to assume that their problem is fear and then go looking for what they're afraid of. That can be difficult, for we're often in denial that we're in the grip of fear.

I have been on a search-and-destroy mission the last ten years to identify, expose, and overcome the fear in my life. I assume it's there and I simply need the courage and God's help to face it and move on. I've written a lot of books, but I'm still afraid to write, thinking that it won't be good or no one will read or buy what I write. I have to battle that fear if I'm going to write the next book. I procrastinate on things (and you do, too) because I'm fearful I'll start incorrectly, or I won't have time to do it well.

I've written extensively in *The Monday Memo* on fear, so let's look at a few *Memos* to see if they can help you admit you're afraid (probably terrified is more like it) and then get free to act and step out.

*****

Monday Memo 768

I received two emails from people who are

considering enlisting my services as a writing coach. Both emails were filled with fear as the people shared their fear of writing about themselves (fear of pride), of paying for the services (fear that God won't provide), and of whether or not their material was good enough to publish (fear of failure and inadequacy). One email talked about how it took all week to follow up on our initial correspondence due to "cold feet."

I've written in the past that the creative process is fraught with fear from beginning to end, and my experience of working with creative people the last few years has done nothing to change that conclusion. I'm no longer surprised when I find fear in my own life, but instead I go looking for it, sort of like conducting a search-and-destroy military mission. I know my enemy is in there somewhere; I just have to find out where in my thinking my fear and shame are hidden and camouflaged.

Why are we so riddled with fear? There is a biblical answer and it's found in Genesis 3:7-10:

> Then the eyes of both of them were opened, and they realized they were naked; so they sewed fig leaves together and made coverings for themselves. Then the man and his wife heard the sound of the Lord God as he was walking in the garden in the cool of the day, and they hid from the Lord God among the trees of the garden. But the Lord God called to the man, "Where are you?" He answered, "I heard you in the garden, and I was afraid because I was naked; so I hid."

Adam and Eve were afraid and ashamed of being exposed, so they hid from God. It's ludicrous for them to think they could hide from God, but they tried, and you and I try to hide as well. Adam and Eve covered themselves with fig leaves – flimsy coverings that would wither and die in a day or two – but we use flimsy excuses to hide our fear and shame. Those excuses sound quite rational, but they're nothing but fig leaves in our minds to mask the terror we face when we consider doing something creative or new.

You may be nodding your head in agreement as you read this *Memo*. Yet, you can be in agreement and still be steeped in and paralyzed by your own fears, denying their existence. Or perhaps you've learned to manage your fears by sticking to the beaten path of life, careful not to veer off into the jungle of the unknown, where you've never been before. Until you take that path less trodden, you won't have to face or even be conscious of your fears.

What's more, if you can wrap your fear in spiritual-sounding excuses, phrases like, "It's not the right season," or "the Lord hasn't released me," or "I'm waiting on a confirmation," then you can comfortably learn to live with your fear, convinced that it's God's will that you be content with your daily routine, medicating your mind with thoughts of what you'll do "one day."

My dear friends, *this* is the day that the Lord has made. You aren't guaranteed tomorrow, so I urge you to face your fears today and move forward. We're children of Adam and Eve, and we all must take steps to emerge from the bushes of fear and shame so we can show forth the fullness of the glory that's ours in Christ. If we don't take those steps, then we'll live a life far below what God had in mind when He sent Jesus to die for our sins. The choice is yours: How will you choose to live today?

*****

Then let's look at another *Memo* that addresses another example of fear from the Old Testament.

Monday Memo 880

In this *Memo*, I have one final thought about mankind's resistance to the call to step out and do whatever it is God has spoken. While the refusal to go is based in people's rebellion against God and His authority, its roots are in fear, and that's why I have titled this week's entry, "The Fear Factor." Let's look at that concept now.

The Refusals

I can think of two cases where people refused when God told them to do something. The first was Jonah, the reluctant prophet, who was told to go to Nineveh and deliver a hard word that God's judgment was coming. Instead of heading to Nineveh, Jonah got on a ship and went in the opposite direction. He eventually revealed that he didn't want to go because he knew the Lord would relent of His verdict if the people repented – which they did and He did. Jonah ended up going, but it was through the whale express that transported him to a spot within walking distance of his assigned destination.

The second refusal was on the part of the

apostles. They heard Jesus' words to go the ends of the earth. The apostles, a title which means 'sent forth ones,' chose to stay in their Jerusalem comfort zone. It took persecution for them to get up and go. They prove it's no guarantee that we'll go or do just because we've heard from the Lord, something that many people claim to be true: "If only God would speak to me, *then* I would know and do His will."

Jonah was afraid God would change His mind, and Jonah wanted Nineveh, the enemies of his people, to be wiped out. The apostles were afraid of what their fellow Jews would say when they went to the Gentiles, so they didn't go, even with their marching orders in hand. The most significant refusal, however, is found in the Old Testament and we can learn important lessons by examining it more closely.

A Tower and a City

The Lord told Adam and Eve, and then Noah, to be fruitful and fill the earth. God wanted them to go and spread out, but their descendants rebelled and stayed put. In Genesis 11, we read that the people decided to make a name for themselves, so they settled down to build a monument or tower to give themselves an identity and place they could call their own.

What did the Lord do when they refused to go? First, he confused their language and then,

> "The Lord scattered them from there over all the earth, and they stopped building the city. That is why it was called Babel— because there the Lord confused the

language of the whole world. From there the Lord scattered them over the face of the whole earth" (Genesis 11:8-9).

This refusal to go was revisited and reversed at Pentecost in Acts 2 when God once again intervened, this time to give mankind a language of the Spirit that would restore their ability to obey God and go. As they went, the Spirit would this time aid their communication as evidenced by every man present in Acts 2 hearing God being extolled in their native tongue. Whereas before, God had confused their language, this time He would clarify it, so they could overcome a major barrier to going and that was the inability to communicate.

The people who built the tower were afraid. They were afraid to go out for whatever reason. Perhaps they were afraid they would lose their identity. Maybe they were fearful of what they would find as they went. They were willing to make bricks in the desert, adding heat to an already unbearable climate, just so they would not have to go.

Are you doing the same thing? Are you making bricks in the desert with people you don't understand (and who don't understand you)? Has God confused the communication between you and others because you're in the wrong place? Is all this rooted in the fear factor that if you go, you'll somehow lose something instead of gaining? When I say go, it doesn't mean you have to go far away (although you may). It does mean you must be in motion to take the initiative on what God has put in your heart to do. Where's the fear factor keeping you from going and doing?

I advise you to consider where you are and where God wants you to be. If they're not the same, then your work and way are probably hard. If you go, whether it's to go and write, go and speak, go and learn, go and build, go and proclaim, or go and create, then God will go with you and you'll experience the true power of Pentecost. God will help you and it will be exhilarating. Your message will be clear because you are clear.

May the Lord reveal to you what your *go* is and then may you face and overcome your fear and obey, knowing that He will be with you to the ends of the earth—or to the end of your street, wherever it is He has chosen for you to serve.

*****

God isn't angry that we're afraid, but He does want to set us free. Do you want to be free? Don't answer too quickly, for if you do want freedom, then it will mean an entirely new lifestyle from the one you have now, which is marinated in fear. And don't be too quick to quote a verse found in 2 Timothy 1:7: "For God hath not given us the spirit of fear; but of power, and of love, and of a sound mind." Why do I say don't be hasty to take refuge in and comfort from that verse? I say that because of what it says in verse six: "For this reason I remind you to fan into flame the gift of God, which is in you through the laying on of hands."

The context of the admonition not to be afraid is in stirring up the gift of God in you. Your greatest fear (and the greatest need for power, love, and a sound mind) will be when you attempt to express your purpose and creativity – it's in your gift, especially if it has been recognized by others through prayer and prophecy. Your enemy will try to use fear to keep you hidden away so you won't fulfill God's plan and we're all too often willing accomplices.

Don't delay any longer and deprive the world of the blessing of your presence and purpose. Be free and flow in the creativity God has placed inside you. If you're going to do God's will, why not now? Do you think it will be any easier in ten years? Are you guaranteed life and health that far in advance? No, this is the day, as I stated above, and I implore you to step out of your fear and into your purpose. You'll be glad you did and the world will be a better place for it.

CONCLUSION

John Stanko

There you have my contribution to this collaboration called *Your Purpose Journey: Embrace the Process*. I should mention that this book is the result of a word the Lord spoke to me in 2018. I was driving along listening to music and realized how many duets I have in my iTunes library, mostly of a man and a woman singing. The Lord whispered to me to "sing duets" and I knew right away that I was to produce some books with female partners. One was with my friend and colleague, Pastor Yvonne Brooks in the UK, and now this one with my best student in the world, Irene Mureithi.

As we were going to press, Irene launched her latest purpose venture, the TKC Show on YouTube and I was a guest for the fourth episode. Two things I mentioned generated so much feedback that Irene asked if I would add some comments about those two subjects as we close this book.

Economic Hardship

The first is the matter of finances. This is the big issue for many people where purpose is concerned, especially if they are already working when they begin their purpose search. The question for many is, "How can I make a living from my purpose? How can I feed my family doing this? Is purpose a luxury only a few can afford to pursue?" Of course, these are good questions, but they actually hinder the pursuit of purpose. Let me explain.

The questions about finances are what I call "how" questions? They are hypothetical questions that consume one's energy and create fear, for the assumption is, "I need my job. If I lose it, my family and I will be poor. We will starve. We will be homeless." We usually don't express our fears in those terms, but the implications are there. The problem is that the person asking the how questions is getting ahead of the process. Before the how comes the what! *What is my purpose?* has to go before *how can I make this work financially?*

I liken people who ask how questions to parents who would decide not to have children because they don't know where they will go to school or what their career will be. Those are how considerations and are impossible to answer at the time a child is born. First, they must have the children and then they can start to address those other questions over time. The what is having children, the how of raising them comes much later and is a process – just like purpose.

I worked with a woman in the UK who was seeking her purpose. She was a nurse and her husband was the pastor of a church. She was really his pastoral assistant, called in her own right, but she was making more money than her husband at her nursing position. So one day, her husband approached me and said, "I really don't want my wife to get too deep into this purpose thing because we need her income." Do you see what he was doing? He was trying to figure out how her purpose was going to work out before they even know what it was!

Eventually, she discovered her purpose, which was to pastor and counsel. Shortly thereafter, she was released from her nursing position and the church grew due to her presence to the point that the church could pay her! That's the power of purpose, but first you have to find out what it is before it can work for you.

However, there are some who find their purpose and set out to make it an income-producing entity right away. Even when God shows you a way to be in purpose and earn revenue, a test will still come to ensure you aren't doing what you do just for the money. What Irene and I saw first and foremost was an opportunity to help people – in the church, marketplace, society, and nations. Then as we moved into the stage where we needed an income to continue, the economic tests came.

Would we continue no matter what? Would we press on and through? We were talking about that phenomenon of the financial testing that comes in the back seat of a taxi, as she related earlier, when I first used the phrase "economic terrorism," explaining, "If the enemy of our souls can't keep us from purpose, he will try to intimidate us to quit. Thus, he uses economic hard times, but God allows him to do so." Now why would God do a thing like that?

We have stated throughout this book that God wants you to know and fulfill your purpose more than you do. Why would He allow the hard times? The best explanation I can come up with is found in Deuteronomy 8:2-5:

> "Remember how the Lord your God led you all the way in the wilderness these forty years, to humble and test you in order to know what was in your heart, whether or not you would keep his commands. He humbled you, causing you to hunger and then feeding you with manna, which neither you nor your ancestors had known, to teach you that man does not live on bread alone but on every word that comes from the mouth of the Lord. Your clothes did not wear out and your feet did not swell during these forty years. Know then in your heart that as a man disciplines his son, so the Lord your God disciplines you."

The suffering cleanses you from impure motives and causes you to know that your ultimate success isn't due to your intelligence, or diligence, or prowess. Your success is because God gave it to you, and the results are to be used as He sees fit. If I had not gone through my hard times, I would never have come to Kenya, which was the only door open to me at the time. God has a way of making His will simple to do and understand, but sometimes we don't like His ways. And this leads to the next concept I want to discuss, which is what Irene has labeled "The Decades."

JOHN STANKO

The Decades

As we publish this book, I am 73 years of age. Now that I am older, I have a lot more life to look back on and reflect. What's more, I have coached enough people in their thirties, forties, and fifties to be able to help them embrace the process that accompanies purpose. Remember, *Embrace the Process* is the byline for this book.

When someone comes to me and let's say they are 45 years old, they usually have an expectation, even a nagging worry, that they should be farther along their purpose journey then they are. They are often educated professionals, who have achieved many career objectives, and have a family and children, along with financial responsibilities like school fees and a house note. But they often think, "I am old now. I can't learn new skills; I don't have time and I can't afford it." So they often stick with jobs, which they sometimes hate, because they don't see that they are still growing and developing. It's then that I share with them the summary of my journey decade by decade.

- In my 30s is when I found my purpose, but I had no idea what it meant. I was raising young children, serving as an assistant pastor in a church, and was learning about life and myself. I developed my purpose message, but had no place to share it. This was a decade of discovery and clarity.

- In my 40s, I started to have opportunities to share the purpose message. lost my dream ministry job with Integrity Music, had to move with my family to another city to take a ministry position, and traveled for the first time to Africa, specifically Zimbabwe and then Kenya. It was in this decade that I started to teach and write about purpose and published three books. I earned my first doctorate when I was 45. I started two companies and learned that my 40s were a decade where I had to be delivered from self by learning about service to others.

- In my 50s, I assumed that I would take what I had done and what I knew at that point in my life and start to apply it in a way that would make some money and earn me some significance. To my surprise, my 50s were my greatest growth years! It was in these years when I discovered the principles that set my thinking free from the limitations of the past. I traveled more and wrote about a dozen books in this decade, which I have determined was the decade of my greatest personal growth.

- Then in my 60s, I was more productive than ever. I taught 50 different classes at the university, went back to school and earned my second doctorate when I was 61, and wrote 45 books. I traveled even more and earned more money than ever. I label my 60s my most fruitful years.

- And now I am in my 70s, and there's no time to slow down. I am learning Spanish, now with 12 of my books translated (by others) for distribution to that market. We paid off our home for the first time in our lives (in the first year of the pandemic no less), and I am enjoying my role as a philanthropist, now supporting many causes around the world. I have a school named after me in Kenya, along with some libraries I helped start.

  I'm only three years into this decade, but I am already labeling them my most meaningful. That's because God has prolonged my days and I can take all that I know and have learned and can share it with an online audience of thousands. And I have written 16 books in those first three years.

There is nothing special about these decades where you are concerned. They aren't a blueprint for your life because God will work differently with you than He did with me. My point in sharing this is that purpose is a process that you can't rush. There are no shortcuts to success. But God is the God of our seasons, and if you are faithful to do what you know today, He will lead and guide you into your tomorrow. What's more, He is always aware of what you need. He promised to give you what you need today with the promise that what you need tomorrow will be there.

I hope you have enjoyed this book and I trust there will be others that come forth from my relationship with Irene. My contact information is at the end of the book, and I hope you'll write me to share your purpose story or ask your purpose questions. I never tire of talking about purpose, so you won't bother me at all if you write. In fact, you'll help me fulfill my purpose of creating order out of chaos. Thank you and may God bless your quest for purpose as you connect with Him and other purpose seekers.

And if I had any final words for you as we close, I would say these are it:

THE BEST IS YET TO COME!

ENDNOTES

[1] Laurence Boldt, *How to Find the Work You Love* (New York: Penguin Books, 1996), page 1.

[2] *Ibid.*, page 20.

[3] https://camtaylor.net/2018/06/22/three-most-important-days/

[4] https://en.wikipedia.org/wiki/Trump_University

[5] Peter F. Drucker, *Management Challenges for the 21st Century* (New York: Harper Collins, 1999), page 164.

[6] *Ibid.*, pages 165-167.

[7] Peter F. Drucker, quoted from the Closing Plenary Session of the 1999 Leadership and Management Conference in Los Angeles, California, November 9, 1999.

ABOUT IRENE MUREITHI

Irene Mureithi is a seasoned, passionate and sought after leadership, growth, and life coach who has worked with top professionals since 2010. She has also facilitated capacity-building training sessions for some of the leading brands in Kenya and beyond. Irene is an entrepreneur who has founded several organizations such as PDI [Personal Development Institute], Serian Country Homes, TKC [The Kingdom Connect], and PC [Provision Consortium]

Irene, in partnership with other facilitators, has trained board members, department heads, senior managers, and general staff in various organizations including,

- Co-operative Bank of Kenya
- Family Bank
- Standard Chartered Bank
- APA Insurance
- Jubilee Insurance
- National Council for Population Development
- Unlocking Potential Ltd (Zimbabwe)

- Makerere University (Students)
- University of Nairobi (Students)
- Eco Bank (IWD Talk)
- Kenya Women Microfinance Bank
- Kenya Airways (HODs)
- Kenya Water and Sanitation Civil Society Network
- Strathmore Business School
- Minet Kenya Insurance Brokers
- ABT Associates
- Standard Chartered Bank
- ABSA Bank
- Mwalimu Sacco
- Numberous churches in Kenya and beyond

Irene is best known for facilitating conversations and conducting assessments in the following subjects and has become an authority in these topics over the years:

1. Emotional intelligence in the workplace
2. Self-awareness in teams
3. Change management
4. Leadership and communication in teams
5. Personal development and growth strategies

Irene brings great value to the training rooms because she combines her authenticity with her inspirational nature to energize, motivate, and, more importantly, transform work teams and individuals in order to be more and to do more. She helped introduce the DISC profile system in Kenya and uses it extensively in her coaching work, most recently coaching young people preparing to transition to their university studies.

OTHER TITLES BY IRENE MUREITHI

Royal and Rich Reflections
Jesus Prays for You
Born to Win Teens
Secret Brilliance
Celebrate the Hard Times

ABOUT JOHN STANKO

John Stanko was born in Pittsburgh, Pennsylvania and graduated from Duquesne University where he received his bachelor's and master's degrees in economics. Since then, John has served as an administrator, teacher, consultant, author, and pastor in his professional career. Along the way, he earned a doctor of ministry degree at Reformed Presbyterian Theological Seminary in Pittsburgh.

John has taught extensively on the topics of time management, life purpose, and organization, and has conducted leadership and purpose training sessions throughout the United States and in 50 countries. He is also certified to administer the DISC and other related personality assessments as well as the Natural Church Development profile for churches. In 2006, he earned the right to facilitate for The Pacific Institute of Seattle, a leadership and personal development program, and for The Leadership Circle, a provider of cultural an executive 360-degree profiles. He has authored over eighty books and written for many publications around the world.

John founded a personal and leadership

development company, called PurposeQuest, in 2001 and today travels the world to speak, consult and inspire leaders and people everywhere. From 2001-2008, he spent six months a year in Africa and still enjoys visiting and working on that continent. John has written dozens of books and in 2014 founded Urban Press, a publishing service that helps other authors publish their dreams.

CONTACTS

Kindly reach Irene Mureithi at
info@pdikenya.africa

And follow at
The Kingdom Connect on Facebook.

Keep in touch with John Stanko
www.purposequest.com
www.johnstanko.us
www.stankbiblestudy.com
www.stankomondaymemo.com

or via email at
johnstanko@gmail.com

John also does extensive relief and community development work in Kenya. You can see some of his projects at
www.purposequest.com/donate

Made in United States
Orlando, FL
14 November 2023